Mistress, Mother, Muse

Mistress, Mother, Muse:

An Exploration of the Female in Modern and Contemporary Mediterranean Literature

By

Maria Palaska

Cambridge Scholars
Publishing

Mistress, Mother, Muse:
An Exploration of the Female in Modern and Contemporary Mediterranean Literature

By Maria Palaska

This book first published 2021

Cambridge Scholars Publishing

Lady Stephenson Library, Newcastle upon Tyne, NE6 2PA, UK

British Library Cataloguing in Publication Data
A catalogue record for this book is available from the British Library

ISBN (10): 1-4438-6329-7
ISBN (13): 978-1-4438-6329-2

TABLE OF CONTENTS

INTRODUCTION

This book is an attempt to explore female liminality twentieth-century Mediterranean literary productions through the lens of mythology and more particularly through the comparative discussion of different versions of classical myths. The primary texts have been chosen on the basis of their representations of liminality in relation to the female qualities of motherhood, sexuality and creativity.

For the purposes of my discussion, liminality as a concept is understood as the indefinable and the elusive. The state of liminality as a threshold and transitional stage implies openness and potential, and consequently a liberation from all definitions and demarcations; not simply a state of standby and in-between but a constant reformation and reorientation, a dynamic of redefinition and remoulding. This transcendence, or even defiance, of definitions subsequently suggests an elusiveness and a chimerical quality.

Female liminality is not only represented but also signified in sexuality, motherhood and in literary inspiration and creativity.

The three heroines in the primary texts illustrate representations of the symbolic significance of women in relation to the liminal. Federico García Lorca's heroine in *Yerma* represents an elusive, liminal motherhood, as she is unable to bear her own children and fantasizes about motherhood. In M. Karagatsis's novel, *The Great Chimera*, Marina illustrates the struggle for an elusive sexual fulfilment and finally Idwar al-Kharrat's Alexandrian women in *City of Saffron* and its sequel *Girls of Alexandria*, embody creativity typified in literary inspiration and articulation.

As the book looks at three twentieth-century Mediterranean literary works and explores the notion of female liminality as (re)presented in these works, it attempts to establish the study of modern and contemporary literary productions of the Mediterranean as a dynamic reality and not as a fossil of the past or an exoticized category.

The choice of texts from the Mediterranean is based on the apprehension of a regional as well as a cultural framework. Consequently, the book falls within the scope of mediterranean studies but it is primarily a comparative literary study. The apprehension of the Mediterranean as a literary concept is ambiguous and quite speculative as the term mediterranean studies mostly refers to historical, archaeological and anthropological research of the prehistoric, ancient, medieval and occasionally early modern eras while its legitimacy as a discipline or research area is often doubted.[1]

The term mediterranean studies, inspired by the pioneering and heavily influential work of Fernand Braudel[2], whose research in the first half of the twentieth century covered the disciplines of anthropology, history, geology, human geography, ecology and archaeology, has come to denote the study of the Mediterranean lands and their populations from antiquity up to the middle ages or early modernity and is often identified with classical greek and roman studies wherein the only concerns with literary works are to be found. The notion of the Mediterranean as a distinctive region, not confined to but inclusive of the mare nostrum, is a romantic construct of nineteenth-century geographers and travel writers based on the contrived dichotomy of the rational and hence civilized and powerful North and the temperamental and hence primitive and disadvantaged South.[3] This dichotomy has been enhanced by the coinage of the term *Mediterraneanism* (coined by Michael Herzfeld under the influence of Edward Said) which acquired a pejorative connotation as it has been loaded with colonial and imperial connotations and often viewed as another Orientalism asserting the political, economical and cultural superiority of the North over the "otherness" of the South.

---

[1] Scholars of mediterranean studies in disciplines such as history, anthropology, archaeology and human geography constantly investigate, negotiate and debate the nature, subject matter and disciplinary status of the study of the Mediterranean. Indicative and noteworthy examples of this type of post-Braudelian scholarship are Peregrine Horden's and Nicholas Purcell's *The Corrupting Sea: A Study of Mediterranean History* (Oxford & Massachusetts: Blackwell, 2000), W.V. Harris's (ed.) *Rethinking the Mediterranean*, (Oxford: Oxford University Press, 2005), David Abulafia's *The Great Sea: A Human History of the Mediterranean* (Oxford-New York: Oxford University Press, 2011), Ian Chambers's *Mediterranean Crossings: The Politics of an Interrupted Modernity* (Durham, N.C.: Duke University Press, 2008) and Matvejevic Predrag's *Mediterranean: A Cultural Landscape*, trans. Michael Henry Heim (Berkeley: University of California Press, 1999).

[2] It is in fact in his work *The Mediterranean and the Mediterranean World in the Age of Philip* II first published in 1949 where the idea of unity and distinctiveness of the Mediterranean and its significance as an area of scholarly research was brought up. His book *Memory and the Mediterranean* is based on the same idea of distinctiveness and unity of the Mediterranean.

[3]As Horden points out while referring to *The Corrupting Sea:* "The idea of the Mediterranean as a *region*, of the circum-Mediterranean *lands* as a distinctive collectivity, is a creation of nineteenth-century thought: it did not arise earlier. It is, most obviously, a creation of nineteenth-century geographers who represent, whether explicitly or indirectly, the Mediterranean ambitions and designs of northern European powers." (Horden 2005, 26-27)

(Harris 2005b, 1-42 and Horden 2005, 26-27)[4] Romanticism has treated the Mediterranean as a literary topos, based precisely on this artificial dichotomy between the North and the South.

The threefold "sin" of Mediterraneanism (exoticizing, homogenizing and restricted comparativism) has not deterred the rising interest in mediterranean studies yet this interest is still confined to the study of the past. The academic study of the modern and contemporary Mediterranean is restricted to social, political, commercial and lately artistic (mostly pertaining to music) relationships within Mediterranean countries.

While archaeologists, historians and ethnographers can theorize about the geographical, ecological, and commercial links (or the *connectivity* as Horden and Purcell refer to them)[5] in antiquity and up to the middle ages, which qualify for the study of the Mediterranean as a field in itself, there is no conceptual framework for the literary scholar or academic who might want to study the twentieth-century and/or contemporary literary productions of the Mediterranean. In other words, the study of the Mediterranean has been dominated by the social sciences as well as antiquity and the middle ages.

Contemporary Mediterranean literature, though, is dynamic[6] as it constantly challenges cultural and national demarcations and offers a superb and uniquely rich canvas for comparative literary analysis.

The study of contemporary literary productions of the Mediterranean that I propose is therefore the exploration of this ever-changing canvas.

It is within this framework that the book examines how liminal female qualities such as motherhood, and sexuality are treated thematically by three

---

[4] Horden and Purcell write:

> The sin of 'Mediterraneanism', [as presented by Said and Herzfeld] can be summarized under three headings. First, it involves *exoticizing*: the label 'Mediterranean' serves the interests of anthropologists studying southern Europe because they feel vulnerable to the charge of operating too close to home for discomfort...The second element in Mediterraneanism is thus *homogenizing*: the discipline has to be validated by exaggerating the uniformity of its chosen area, usually by recourse to vaguely defined cultural traits...The assumption of homogeneity, thirdly, determines the *restricted comparativism* that is typical of Mediterraneanists. A priori, comparison across the sea, between Christendom and Islam, is essential - whether relevant to the matter or not. (Horden and Purcell 2000, 486-487)

[5] See Horden and Purcell 2000, 123-172 for their definition and discussion of connectivity as well as Purcell 2003, 9-11

[6] Or an "open itinerary" to borrow an expression originally used for comparative literature as a discipline. See Guillen 1993, 4.

twentieth-century male authors of the Mediterranean basin.[7] Ultimately, the book seeks to illustrate the transcendental perspective through which these liminal aspects are discussed.

The book draws upon myth as a theoretical perspective and more particularly upon its inherent transformative quality, which is termed *potency* and which is schematically represented in an algorithmic model. The work of Hans Blumenberg and Ernst Cassirer is of fundamental significance in any consideration of the grounding of mythic potency; the concepts of *fundamental* vis-à-vis m as well as the *law of metamorphosis* and *consanguinity* in myth accommodate the grounding of potency and its significance for literary discussion. Myth as a tool for literary analysis is therefore suggested as an alternative theory.

The methodology employed is comparative, understood as "the systematic study of supranational assemblages" (Guillen 1993, 3) and as the exploration of the tensions between the particular and the general, the singular and the plural (ibid., 5-23). The primary as well as secondary texts are discussed independent of their national and cultural milieu, although this is considered when necessary.

Comparative discussion in this book is in no way confined to the "restricted comparativism" that Horden and Purcell attribute to Mediterraneanists. It is primarily a comparison of texts and not of national, ideological or cultural modes.

Ultimately, this book suggests an alternative way of looking at literary analysis, myth and women in literature.

---

[7] Idwar al-Kharrat might as well be considered a twenty-first and hence contemporary author as he is still alive and active as an author.

CHAPTER ONE

MYTH AND TEXTUAL ANALYSIS

1. The dynamics of myth

Myth often constitutes the main axis of a literary text or the occasion for its birth and development. It is usually apprehended as narrative (drawing upon the Aristotelian definition of μύθος as plot) and is consequently classified as a literary genre.[8] Mythic symbols, figures and patterns often appear in literary works, playing a major or minor (though not necessarily insignificant) role, and the influence of a particular myth on a writer as well as the conscious rewriting of a myth or the creation of a new myth, mythopoeia, have been a common phenomenon throughout literary history.

The question of whether myth is literature, and the factors that determine this identification, is an interesting yet complicated matter which is worth addressing but almost impossible to resolve in a definite manner and does not fall within the scope of this Chapter.[9]

This Chapter, and indeed the book in its entirety, present an argument for the use of myth as an independent tool for literary analysis. More particularly, they illustrate the employment of mythic notions, symbols, patterns and images within the context and practice of literary analysis, with the objective of achieving an enlightened and enlightening interpretation of the literary text(s) in question.[10] The employment of mythic elements as

---

[8] Since the Eleatic School of Presocratic philosophy, myth was seen as a preparatory stage for logos (λόγος), as an allegory which was a "cloak for a speculative, scientific, or ethical truth." (Cassirer 1964, 2) It was actually Schelling who first argued for a tautegorical interpretation of myths and attempted to liberate myth from the tyranny of the allegorical, figurative approach. (ibid.,1-26 and Meletinsky 1998, 3-4)

[9] Robert Segal is not only sceptical regarding the very concept of myth studies as an academic and scholarly field but he also contends that because of the absence of a single, agreed, definition of myth, the study of myth is a mere extension of other disciplines. (Segal 2004, 2)

[10] For the purposes of this book I dispense with the already established approaches to myth such as structuralism, semantics, anthropology, psychoanalysis and history which have imposed their own agendas on mythic analysis.

tools for literary analysis differs significantly from their mere detection in literary works as well as from the study of the influence of a myth on a literary text, or the discussion of modern myths in the works of poets, novelists and dramatists. While all the aforementioned have proved to be unquestionably beneficial to literary discussion, they are founded upon the premise of a direct influence between literary text and myth and, in essence, of an ostensible kinship between the two (which might consist of a conscious retelling or adaptation of a myth, the presence of mythic symbols, allusions, characters, etc.), or of what Northrop Frye calls "displacement" (Ziolkowski 1996, 252) and Mircea Eliade "degeneration" of myth into literature (ibid., 256).

The most significant factor problematizing the already complex and intricate relationship between myth and literature is the lack of scholarly and academic consensus on a single, comprehensive definition of myth. As Stambovsky notes, "'myth' itself is now so broadly and disparately defined that the very intelligibility of 'myth as *a collective term*' is a topic of debate." (Stambovsky 1996, 24) The definitions of myth vary significantly, and usually they reflect a particular approach to the study of mythology.[11] The lack of a single, accepted definition of myth subsequently puts the existence of the study of myth as an academic and scholarly field into question. The primary definition of myth, chronologically as well as conceptually, is its antithesis to reason as encountered in the proverbial controversy between λόγος (logos) and μύθος (mythos), between what came to be regarded as Cartesian rationality and primal, underdeveloped thinking, in other words, between what has been perceived as uncontaminated reason and tainted myth. This controversy, initiated by the Presocratics, has resulted in a negative predisposition towards the study of myth. An indicative consequence of this negative predisposition is the use of the word myth in today's common parlance as something untrue, illogical, fallacious and fictitious. This view continued to exercise a great influence in the study

[11] Approaches to myth expand across different disciplines and they involve eminent scholars and intellectuals. Sir James Frazer is, perhaps, the most influential figure (though often severely criticized), due to the breadth of his research and his pioneering work. Along with Jane Harrison they form the Cambridge school of the ritualistic approach to myth. Bronislaw Malinowski pioneered the socio-anthropological view on myth which takes into account socio-economic parameters. Lévi-Strauss represents the structuralist approach while the Jungian Kerenyi is a follower of the psychoanalytic/archetypal approach, although the strictly archetypal perspective is attributed to Northrop FryeAll these approaches gravitate towards a definition of myth which reflects their own basic premise; the Cambridge school, for instance, understands myth as a narrative emerging out of the necessity to complement rituals.

of myth, even when other disciplines such as psychoanalysis, structuralism and semantics were introduced into mythic analysis. Eminent theorists of myth and literary critics, such as Sir James Frazer, Jane Harrison, Northrop Frye, Bronislaw Malinowski, Mircea Eliad, and Claude Lévi -Strauss, failed or refused to accept the autonomy of myth and, more particularly, its independence from narrative and literary discourse.[12] Myth, therefore, is usually perceived and referred to as a branch of literary or philosophical studies or as a by-product of literary production.

Given the problematics of a definition of myth and its relationship to literature, it is indeed a challenge to approach myth from a strictly philosophic point of view (where myth is subject to philosophic enquiry) attempting thus to explore its nature and essence while liberating it from any manner and form of dependence and advocating its autonomy.[13]

Myth's autonomy emanates from its inherent dynamic quality manifested in the state of process which Ernst Cassirer names "Becoming" and believes is inextricably related to primordiality or what he calls *ἀρχή*.[14] Cassirer understands the relationship between myth and ἀρχή in conjunction with Schelling's philosophical perspective on myth as tautegorical and argues that myth as a stage of human consciousness involves a process which he calls "theogonic". This is a key word that integrates two basic mythic concepts related to ἀρχή: divinity (θεός) and origin (γένεσις).[15] In other

---

[12] Also see Douglas 1996, 68-78

[13] However, even the term philosophy of myth turns out to be problematic as it relegates to the perennial opposition between philosophy as systematic methodology representing reason and myth as a pre-rational, anarchic terrain representing primitive thought. It is actually Schelling who articulates very vehemently the disparity of the term philosophy of myth as a challenge and an occasion for a more serious and systematic exploration of the relationship between philosophy and myth. (Schelling 1995, 50-57)

[14] Cassirer actually bypasses the μύθος-λόγος binary by acknowledging the concept of ἀρχή as a liminal stage between myth and philosophy. "It (ἀρχή) designates the zone between myth and philosophy–but a boundary which as such partakes of both the spheres it divides, representing the point of difference between the mythical concept of the beginning and the philosophical concept of the 'principle'." (Cassirer 1964, 1-2)

[15] It is very important here to explain the exact meaning of the word γένεσις. Γένεσις is the noun of the verb γίγνομαι which means to become, to happen but also to be, to be born. Its synonyms are ποιοῦμαι (to be created) and γεννόμαι (to be born). The verb γίγνομαι has the same root as the verb γεννῶ which means to beget (for father) and to bear (for mother, to beget for mother is τίκτω). Consequently, γένεσις incorporates the concepts of birth as well as origin and creation. However, in order to understand the creative seminal nature of myth it is important to highlight the fact that γένεσις as birth refers to creation and not to labour.

words, this "theogonic" process is the process of creation of the beginnings (Cassirer 1964, 6). As Cassirer articulates it, "The mythological process is the process of the truth re-creating and so realizing itself." (ibid., 7) affirming thus the tautegorical quality of myth and its independence.

Cassirer bases this process on his view of myth as "an independent configuration of man's consciousness" (ibid., 3) which is not to be understood in terms of an outside, but as something self-referential confirming Kant's Copernican revolution (Scarborough 1994, 20-21). In other words, myth is defined in terms of its intrinsic qualities and not as antithetical, complementary or analogous to any other form or discipline. In fact, for Cassirer, myth is a world in itself, "uniquely a complete human world, with its own type of perception, action, and 'explanations' of reality." (Schultz 2000, 117) Cassirer draws upon Schelling's view on myth as tautegorical and as a process within human consciousness, arguing that "all attempts to intellectualise myth – to explain it as an allegorical expression of a theoretical or moral truth – have failed." (Cassirer 1945, 81) The failure of the allegorical apprehension of myth signifies the inadequacy and ineffectiveness of the dependence of myth on an outside and inevitably calls for a serious consideration of the autonomy and intrinsic worth of myth. The keywords in understanding and delineating such an apprehension of myth are: autonomous, self-referential, dynamic, inherently transformative.

The state of "Becoming" which characterizes and determines myth, is what I would like to call *mythic potency* and it entails progress and evolution. For the purposes of this Chapter and book, mythic potency is best represented with the assistance of the mathematical concept of an algorithm as a way of providing a new perception of myth based on concrete processes, and free from enigmatic and often problematic theoretical discourses.

The mathematical definition of algorithm is that of "a set of instructions that can be mechanically executed in a finite amount of time in order to solve some problems" (Gersting 1998, 13). An algorithm can be functional but it can also be descriptive: in other words, it is a process based on a sequence of steps in order to test a hypothesis or describe relationships.

The process of the evolution of a particular myth is traced in a series of essential and sine qua non elements of the myth which signify the algorithmic pattern. The following section of this Chapter illustrates how myth incorporates sequence and progression towards several different orientations, and it does so intrinsically and is therefore *potent.*

For Cassirer this potency is permeated by a form of mythic transformation which connotes change and mobility (Cassirer 1945, 81). More particularly, he argues that despite myth being "refractory to a merely logical analysis" (ibid., 72), there is one feature or law which governs the mythical world, and that is the "law of metamorphosis"(ibid., 81) which suggests the absence of demarcations and categories by virtue of a perennial flux in which "everything may be turned into everything." (ibid.) According to Cassirer, the mythical world is characterized by continuity, motion, and what he calls "consanguinity" (ibid., 82). This consanguinity is the underlying thread that links all the different metamorphoses of a myth. It is in fact a kinship based on vital, creative elements in the same way that relatives share the same genetic material although they are different in all other respects. Cassirer acknowledges and defends vehemently the dynamic nature of myth: "It is now generally admitted that it is a very inadequate conception of myth and magic to look upon them as typically aetiological or explanatory. We cannot reduce myth to certain fixed static elements; we must strive to grasp it in its inner life, in its mobility and versatility, in its dynamic principle." (ibid., 76) This consanguinity is a property that qualifies myth to be dynamic and versatile and eventually to be subject to metamorphosis.

The idea behind the concept of algorithms is a sequential process which not only implies progression but also entails a dynamic state. As such, the algorithmic model qualifies for an effective schematic representation of mythic Becoming and potency. The algorithmic model, which involves a process based on a pattern, echoes the notion of "patterned action" of myth, which allows myth to function as "a useful tool for literary and cultural analysis":

> …myth as a useful tool for literary and cultural analysis is understood as a complex image used in a symbolic manner which by means of a simple narrative explains man's relation to his fellows, his society, his environment, his destiny. Without at least the vestiges of narrative we have only a symbol. A symbol may condition response, but only a myth patterns action. And it is the potential of patterned action that makes myth a fundamental concept in the study of a society through the medium of its literary remains. (Boewe 1961, 196)

Boewe argues that the study of myth from a specific culture or society enables us to understand the literary products of this society and eventually understand the society itself,[16] but a departure from this strictly anthropological and sociological approach allows for the assertion of the autonomy of myth and its emancipation from other disciplines. A focus on the "potential of

---

[16] Boewe's view on myth, therefore, is essentially anthropological and sociological despite his own claims that it is a view on myth as a means of literary analysis.

patterned action" (ibid.) of myth reveals the full mythic potential for transformation, which can be of great use to literary analysis.[17]

Hans Blumenberg in his book *Work on Myth* makes a distinction between *fundamental* and *original* myth, the original myth being a first, completed version and fundamental myth containing the essential parts that remain throughout the various alterations: "The fundamental myth is not what was pre-given, but rather what remains visible in the end, what was able to satisfy the receptions and expectations" (Blumenberg 1990, 174-175). In other words, the fundamental myth is the distilled form that can survive various alterations and transformations. Interestingly, there is a further correspondence between myth and algorithms as the notion of the fundamental myth approximates the Greatest Common Divisor of the Euclidean algorithm. The Euclidean algorithm is a sequence of divisions, and specifically "A procedure in which each operation depends on the results of the preceding operation" in order to find the Greatest Common Divisor (Merritt 1962, 7). Based on this idea of divisions, mathematicians came up with the so-called "Divide-And-Conquer" algorithm, in which a problem is broken down to smaller subproblems (Gersting 1998, 149). In a similar manner, the transformation of a myth can be broken down to smaller steps consisting of alterations in particular mythic elements. Metamorphosis is, in fact, a transformation that the original myth undergoes, and what Blumenberg calls the fundamental myth is the sediment of a series of such transformations.

The capacity of myth to expand, multiply and evolve is intrinsic and forms an essential element of mythic consciousness. *Potency* corresponds to the inherent potentiality, the energy that can initiate a sequential, evolutionary process. *Potency* is the dynamics of myth. Yet, this dynamic quality is also the liminality of myth as a process of "Becoming."

Cassirer clearly acknowledges this potential and his understanding is close to the idea of potency.

> For nowhere in myth do we find a passive contemplation of things; here all contemplation starts from an attitude, an act of the feeling and will. Insofar as myth condenses into lasting configuration, insofar as it sets before us the stable outlines of an objective world of forms, the significance of this world becomes intelligible to us only if behind it we can feel the dynamic of the life feeling from which it originally grew. Only where this feeling is aroused

[17] John Vickery (1996, 297) acknowledges the significance of myth in literary criticism and argues that: "An awareness of myth enables the critic to isolate latent elements, which, like those of dreams, possess the force that vitalizes the manifest pattern." However, he does not discuss this significance but dwells on the description and analysis of the relationship between myth and literature.

> from within, only where it manifests itself in love and hate, fear and hope, joy and grief, is that mythical fantasy engendered which creates a world of specific representations. But from this it seems to follow that any characterization of the mythical forms of thought applies only to something mediated and derived – that it must remain inadequate unless it succeeds in going back from the mere mythical form of *thought* to the mythical form of *intuition* and its characteristic form of *life*. (Cassirer 1964, 69-70)

Evidently, Cassirer perceives this force behind myths that is related to life itself and he also acknowledges a disposition of the recipients of myth towards the recognition of this life. He calls this disposition *will* and he denounces a passive and sterile apprehension of myth.[18]

The words *life* and *will* echo Henri Bergson's élan vital and his biological philosophy. Bergson acknowledges a force in nature, which dictates progress and forward movement (Bergson 1935, 100-105). Like Cassirer, Bergson resorts to nature in order to illustrate successfully the genuiness and legitimacy of his thesis. His term élan vital is close to my notion of potency.

Myth, however, does not fully depend on philosophy and philosophical discourse in the same manner that it does not fully depend on literature. Neither does its opposition to philosophy as a manner of systematic methodology (the opposition between λόγος and μύθος) suggest an impossibility for philosophical truth in myth. The mythic world and consciousness are and should be seen as yet another domain, another discourse which cannot be a priori stigmatized as fallacious and illegitimate only by virtue of being different and of having been confronted as an "Other".[19]

H. and H.A. Frankfort (1948, 7) also subscribe to the idea of the dynamic nature of myth and acknowledge an even more forceful agent in myth which they call "compelling authority." According to them

> It is essential that true myth be distinguished from legend, saga, fable, and fairy tale. All these may retain elements of the myth. And it may also happen that a baroque or frivolous imagination elaborates myths until they become

---

[18] Cassirer's approach to myth has been criticized and dismissed by G.S Kirk as arbitrary and as referring to religion and not myth. However, Kirk himself does not provide a sound theoretical refutation of Cassirer's argument or an alternative view. See Kirk 1973, 261-268.

[19] Dimitra Mitta (1997, 256-257) suggests two alternative ways of looking at myth: either as a continuation of the project of the Enlightment (i.e. to reveal the meaning behind what seems to be fallacious – fallacious here does not imply untrue) or as a completion of what Habermas has called the "uncompleted project" of modernism.

> mere stories. But true myth presents its images and its imaginary actors, not with the playfulness of fantasy, but with a compelling authority. It perpetuates the revelation of a 'Thou'. (ibid.)

Myth therefore possesses a power to reveal truth, a truth which is not a mere object, an "It", but a "Thou" and as such it is unique. (ibid., 3-6) Moreover, this "compelling authority" is an active quality which enables myth to create and re-create itself yet the term is quite strong as it implies control and imposition whereas potency suggests freedom and ingenuity.

> Myth, then, is to be taken seriously, because it reveals a significant, if unverifiable, truth-we might say a metaphysical truth. But myth has not the universality and the lucidity of theoretical statement. It is concrete, though it claims to be inassailable in its validity. It claims recognition by the faithful; it does not pretend to justification before the critical. (ibid.)

In short, myth is an independent and dynamic configuration of human consciousness with an intrinsic transformative impulse. The use of the concept of potency and its algorithmic representation is an attempt to find a more concrete way of presenting and at the same time exploring the versatility of myth.

It is precisely this "Becoming", this inherent potential for evolution and transformation which renders myth autonomous, dynamic and versatile and qualify it as an alternative tool for literary analysis. One of the main aims of this book is to argue for the use of latent mythic qualities in explicating texts that have no manifest connection with the myth in question.

The following pages are an illustration of mythic metamorphosis and of the dynamics of myth.

2. Mythic potency and its significance in comparative literary discussion

This section looks at the myth of Medea as an example of the exploration and illustration of the dynamics of myth. The versions of the myth that are discussed in relation to mythic transformation are Euripides's play *Medea,* Seneca's play *Medea* and Christa Wolf's novel *Medea*. The choice of these texts is based on the distinctive manner in which they develop the myth in question. The following flow chart serves as a schematic representation of the transformation of the myth of Medea in the three aforementioned versions through an algorithmic sequential process.

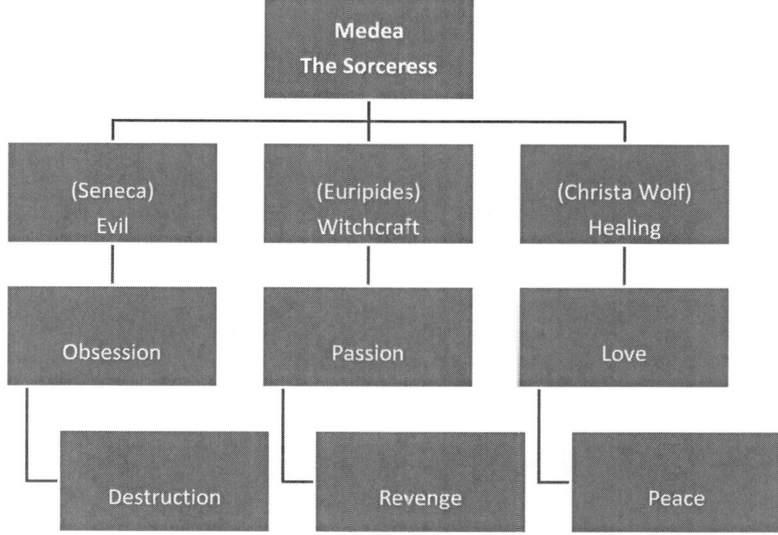

Sorcery is the vital element without which the myth of Medea cannot exist. The concept of sorcery itself encompasses a wide range of practices, predispositions and qualities (the distinction between white and black magic is an obvious example) and is therefore open to various orientations. Once the element of sorcery is given a specific orientation then new elements can be added to the particular version of the myth. The conclusion of the myth varies according to the preceding alterations. There is in fact an input-output relationship which is reminiscent of the mathematical input-output relationship found in algorithms.

While the Euripidean version renders a Medea who is tormented by her passion for Jason and employs her witchcraft to take revenge on him for abandoning her, Seneca's Medea is a far more wicked and disturbed female who is obsessed with Jason and uses her wickedness in order to cause utter catastrophe not only in Jason's life but in her own as well. Finally, Christa Wolf's version assumes a completely different stance and presents Medea as a healer who loves Jason deeply and who eventually becomes victimized and sycophantically outcasted by the society she lives in.

Euripides's *Medea* is not, in fact, the first record of the story of Medea but is based on earlier tales and narratives; however, it is considered a seminal text in the study of the myth of Medea as it is the first organized, officially recorded account of the story of Medea and can thus be considered the original myth concerning Medea. The acknowledgement of the

Euripidean text as an original myth allows the detection of elements that are in a seminal state (such as the notion of sorcery) and of elements that have been developed by Euripides but are still open to reworkings (such as the passion for Jason). The potential for reworking, which realizes itself in the versions of Seneca and Wolf, is what I have earlier termed mythic potency. An example of an element which exists in the Euripidean tragedy in a latent state is Medea's intelligence and high perception which underlies the notion of sorcery and which in Euripides connotes witchcraft, in Seneca manifestation of evil and in Wolf benevolent healing properties.

In Euripides's version, sorcery is associated with witchcraft. Medea is portrayed as an Asian sorceress who possesses the art of witchcraft and is involved in the world of the occult. Medea is a vehicle for the darkness and gloominess of the Orient which is juxtaposed to the radiance of the Hellenic world. She represents the Dionysian world of the supernatural, totally oblivious to Apollonian rationality. As she remarks "It is best to go by the straight road, the one in which I am most skilled, and make away with them by poison, so be it then." (Euripides 1958, 38) She is a skilful witch and an ally of Hecate, the lunar goddess of darkness and the supernatural. The "straight road" for her is the obscure and unintelligible world of the occult.

However, it is not Medea's sorcery per se that plays a primary role in the play as it is not a key concept that can justify her actions. On the contrary, sorcery is a background element necessary for the narratological as well dramaturgical development of the play. Sorcery is related to revenge, and is used by Medea as the most efficient way for her to take revenge on Jason. Medea resorts to her witchcraft after careful reasoning and after considering other options that do not eventually seem suitable for her. Sorcery is a means for Medea to take revenge on Jason, a vehicle for her bitterness and anger. As D.L. Page points out in the Introduction to the Oxford University Press edition of *Medea*, "At once dry-eyed and calculating she reasons in measured sentences the way of her revenge" (1988, xviii). Medea does not murder her children because she is a sorceress but because she wants to punish Jason. From that point of view Medea is not the ruthless mother who murders her children but a very clever woman who carefully plans her revenge and uses her skills in order to achieve the best results for her plan. Ruth Morse (1996, 31) commenting on Diana Rigg's 1994 performance of Euripides's *Medea,* mentions the rationality that the actress manages to convey with respect to Medea's deed of revenge. "There was a fatalism about her act which was perceived as a choice already made, and nothing mad or emotionally extravagant about the doing of it." Indeed, Euripides's emphasis is not so much on witchcraft and occultist practices but rather on the woman Medea, her wounded pride, her mind, and her “choice already made”. It is also worth mentioning that Medea is in fact a pharmakis, namely a practitioner of white magic involving charms, incantations, drugs and that pharmakis was not an unsual practice in fifth-century Athens. According to Bernard Knox (1979, 308-309) it is the use of poison that has led to the dark, negative image of Medea and the Euripidean Medea has no supernatural powers whatsoever while her only weapons are her cunning and the poison.

Medea’s intelligence is brought up explicitly by Euripides in her dialogue with Kreon. Kreon is aware of her acute perception and he is scared of her. “You are a clever woman, versed in evil arts” (Euripides 1958, 35) he admits, and later on he explains his fears: “A sharp-tempered woman, or for that matter a man, is easier to deal with than the clever type who holds her tongue. No. You must go.”(ibid., 35-36) Undoubtedly, it is her acute mind and not her temperament that scares him; it is not an explosion of wrath that Kreon fears but the quiet perception and the unmanifested calculations of Medea which he perceives as a threat. At this point we can detect a seed of Christa Wolf’s rendition of Medea as a quiet and perceptive healer and an exceptionally charismatic personality.

Contrary to the prevalent critical approach according to which Euripides’s Medea is a frenzied lunatic, a careful study of the text as an original myth indicates that it is not Medea’s dionysian, maenadic, mystic consciousness but her intelligence which points to sorcery as the most suitable and effective form of revenge. This is extremely significant as it reveals aspects of Medea that contribute to the study of her character while providing material for further progression of the myth. Some of these aspects are Medea’s intelligence, her strong personality and her sanity. The Euripidean text explicitly illustrates Medea’s intelligence in her dialogue with Kreon and in some of Medea’s speeches. An indicative example is her response to Kreon where she admits that she is clever and that she is also considered clever by Corinthian people.

> Οὐ νῦν με πρῶτον, ἀλλά πολλάκις Κρέον,
> ἔβλαψε δόξα μεγάλα τ’ εἴργασται κακά.
> χρὴ δ’ οὔποθ’ ὅστις ἀρτίφρων πεφυκ’ἀνὴρ
> παῖδας περισσῶς ἐκδιδάσκεσθαι σοφούς·
> χωρὶς γὰρ ἄλλης ἧς ἔχουσιν ἀργίας
> φθόνον πρὸς ἀστῶν ἀλφάνουσι δυσμενῆ.
> σκαιοῖσι μὲν γὰρ καινὰ προσφέρων σοφὰ
> δόξεις ἀχρεῖος κοὐ σοφὸς πεφυκέναι
> τῶν δ’ αὖ δοκούντων εἰδέναι τι ποικίλον
> κρείσσων νομισθεὶς ἐν πόλει λυπρὸς φανῇ.
> ἐγώ δὲ καὐτὴ τῆσδε κοινωνῶ τύχης.
> σοφὴ γὰρ οὖσα, τοῖς μέν εἰμ’ ἐπίφθονος,

[τοῖς δ' ἡσυχαία, τοῖς δὲ θατέρου τρόπου,]
τοῖς δ' αὖ προσάντης· εἰμὶ δ' οὐκ ἄγαν σοφή.

(Euripides 1988, 15-16)

> This is not the first time, Kreon. Often previously through being considered clever I have suffered much. A person of sense ought never to have his children brought up to be more clever than the average. For, apart from cleverness bringing them no profit, it will make them objects of envy and ill-will. If you put new ideas before the eyes of fools they'll think you foolish and worthless into the bargain; and if you are thought superior to those who have some reputation for learning, you will become hated. I have some knowledge myself of how this happens; For being clever, I find that some will envy me, others object to me. Yet all my cleverness is not so much. (Euripides 1958, 35)

Euripides clearly attributes to his heroine a great degree of intelligence and the original text suggests that the heroine does not simply possess a cerebral and cognitive intelligence of the kind that can be measured by an IQ or other similar tests. The word chosen by Euripides is σοφὶα (wisdom), which has particular connotations. According to Knox (1979, 313)

> "Clever" is not an adequate translation of *sophe* – but then, there isn't one. It is a word used in the fifth century to describe not only the skill of the artisan and the poet, not only the wisdom won by experience and reflection, but also the new intellectual enlightened outlook of the great sophistic teachers and the generation they had taught. This is why Creon fears her.

In her response to Kreon, the adjective σοφὴ/σοφὸς is repeated five times. Her speech to the king illustrates her self-awareness and articulates her own acknowledgement of the centrality of her wisdom in the issue of her exile. As Morse (1996, 29) observes, "Throughout the play Medea's intelligence (her σοφὶα) is emphasized as a dangerous attribute; it is dangerous because intelligence is power, and she is an intelligent woman. Creon is afraid that she might think of something. This could not sound more rational." This quality of σοφὶα is exploited by Christa Wolf in her novel *Medea* where this general notion of intelligence is transformed into the particular charisma of intuition and healing. Wolf's novel dwells upon the "envy" and "ill-will" that people feel for Medea, and in fact these two elements constitute vital parts of the novel and determine the evolution of the plot.

There is therefore a very interesting paradox which I believe corresponds to the crux of the debate concerning the character of Medea. The allegedly wicked sorceress is at the same time a very intelligent and perceptive person, exhibiting excellent reasoning and argumentation. She also demonstrates an impressive self-awareness and consciousness of her distinctive skills and talents. It is this paradox, this bizarre and inexplicable amalgamation of reason and the supernatural, that has made Medea such a challenging and controversial figure in literature and art. As Marianne McDonald (1997, 303) points out "Medea is a complex being. Following the model of the soul that Plato gives us in *Phaedrus*, with the *λογιστικόν* element (reason) as a charioteer driving the horses *ἐπιθυμητικόν* (desire) and *θυμοειδές* (passion, 264a; cf. Rep. 4.440e for these labels), some see Medea with runaway horses, others as clearly in command. The ostensible contradiction in the Euripidean version, which again asserts the richness and multiplexity of the Medea myth and justifies the text as the original myth, lies in the personality of Medea who is supposedly a Dionysian agent while at the same time possessing Apollonian rationality.

Christiane Sourvinou-Inwood (1997, 253-296) does not consent to the idea of contradiction in the Euripidean Medea but she does acknowledge that Medea possesses incongruous qualities, such as those of a "normal", "good" and "bad" woman. According to her there is a process of alternation, of zooming and distancing from these qualities. The metaphor of zooming and distancing illustrates a vacillation on the part of Euripides concerning the "badness" and "goodness" and the more general "normality" of his heroine. This vacillation is justified later on in this chapter, when Christa Wolf's account of Medea's story is examined. There is a correspondence between the Platonic qualities that McDonald has attached to Medea and the three qualities that Sourvinou-Inwood considers; λογιστικόν corresponds to the goodness, ἐπιθυμητικόν corresponds to the "badness" and θυμοειδές corresponds to the "normality" of the heroine. A woman (or a man for that matter) who acts according to the dictations of reason is classified as "good" because reason, very often referred to as prudence, has been acknowledged as the socially condoned way of behaviour. On the contrary, a person who lives according to the dictations of ἐπιθυμητικόν, is a "bad" person because desire had been stigmatized – primarily by religion and by society – as a harmful and unacceptable emotional experience. Whether "bad" or "good" a person is labelled as "abnormal" if they are overwhelmed by passion, θυμοειδές, and Medea's "abnormality" is intextricably related to her passionate character.

Who is Euripides's Medea after all? Is she the enraged witch or the intelligent woman? Is she a "good" or a "bad" woman? Is she a "normal" woman? Is she the charioteer in command of the horses or is she simply driven by them, having lost all control over her vehicle? Euripides attempted to fuse carefully the existing mythologems, tales and rumours concerning

Medea and enrich them with his own creativity and incisive perception. The result is a heroine who encompasses the Platonic qualities of reason, desire and passion, and this has made the play a concrete and comprehensive work, constituting thus the original myth about Medea. Euripides does not provide a clear representation of either the one or the other profile of his heroine and it is this ambiguity which makes Medea one of the most fascinating figures in world literature, while allowing various reworkings of the myth. As Marianne McDonald (1997, 303) points out about the Euripidean Medea: "She is not simple, and neither are her interpretations. She overflows constricting categories."

Looking at the Euripidean text as the first stage of a sequential process enables the reader to perceive the potential inherent in the character of Medea and so to understand the dynamic nature of the myth, and to reach new understandings of it. In fact, the complexity of the Euripidean Medea stems from the comprehensive nature of the play, and it is actually this complexity and ambiguity of Medea that has enabled and fostered the creation of so many variations of the myth. Euripides's play as an original myth, incorporates elements, such as Medea's intelligence and sorcery and her relationship to Jason, that are open to exploitation and development. Sorcery as witchcraft is simply one way to portray Medea's peculiar nature and her exceptional personality; it is the input which undergoes certain alterations and reaches a conclusion.

In Seneca, however, sorcery is not exhausted in the execution of magical practices: it is the manifestation of evil. More particularly, in Seneca's tragedy Medea's sorcery is not simply a craft, or an exercise of occultism. It is a malicious practice, a result of an evil nature. Seneca portrays Medea is a woman with a great susceptibility to mental upheavals, and it is this susceptibility that enables her to exercise sorcery. Medea is susceptible to malevolent supernatural forces and to chthonic experiences. Her soliloquy, which opens the play, is an evocation to these forces: "Be present, be present, ye goddesses who avenge crime, your hair foul with writhing snakes, grasping the smoking torch with your bloody hands, be present now, such as once ye stood in dread array beside my marriage couch." (Seneca 1960, 229) While, later on, preparing her evil deed Medea asks for help from the realm of darkness. "I supplicate the throng of the silent, and you, funereal gods, murky Chaos and shadowy Dis' dark dwelling-place, the abysses of dismal Death, girt by the banks of Tartarus." (ibid., 291) Unlike the Euripidean heroine, she is not simply seeking revenge but she delves in the deepest and darkest layers of the supernatural world in order to channel the evil that resides inside her. In fact, she sees her crime as a sacrifice to the altar of those chthonic forces, and wishes to pray prior to committing the crime. There is an integration with the world of evil and a subsequent association with the powers and deities representing this world. Unlike Euripides's tragedy, the emphasis here is not on Medea's mind or personality but on her subconscious.

At this point, a slight but significant metamorphosis in the myth of Medea can be detected; this is manifested and exemplified in the idea of sorcery. The mere exercise of magic for the sake of revenge, which we saw in Euripides, becomes a satanic, contaminated consciousness seeking destruction and death. We are beginning to see therefore how the vigour of this particular myth is realizing itself: from a dynamic impulse it is transubstantiated into a concrete reality. What in Euripides is a straightforward revenge – "for this is best to wound my husband" (Euripides 1958, 52) – in Seneca is a consequence of evil: "Does he think that all my powers of evil are so exhausted?" (Seneca 1960, 237) Bernard Knox points out that

> It is in fact, in the Roman poets of the first centuries B.C. and A.D. (Horace, Virgil and Lucan) that something resembling our conception of a witch first appears to give literary shape to the medieval witch of Christian times who serves the devil instead of Hecate but claims the same powers to raise the dead, curse, blight, transform and prophesy. (Knox 1979, 307)

Knox further observes that the Euripidean text does not in any way present a frantic, disturbed or evil Medea: "The term 'witch' with its medieval overtones of black magic, ugliness, and malevolence, has no place in a description of Euripides's Medea." (ibid.)

Medea's original intelligence is transformed into malice by Seneca. His Medea bears no resemblance to the intelligent, rational Euripidean heroine who premeditates and considers revenge as the best form of justice. Seneca's Medea is malicious by nature and is mentally disturbed. She doesn't simply wish to take revenge but to cause destruction and death. In her introductory soliloquy she refers to the "force of madness" that her deeds involve. Kreon fears her cunning: "She is plotting mischief; I know her guile, I know her power. Whom will she spare? Whom will she let live in peace?" (Seneca 1960, 243-245) In Euripides, Kreon acknowledges Medea's clever mind and in fact it is her sharpness that scares him; he does admit that a clever person, either man or woman constitutes a threat to his authority. In Seneca though, Kreon fears Medea's distorted intelligence, her evil mind and her cunning. It is not so much intelligence, as such, that disturbs him, but the consequences of a perverted intelligence is what terrifies him.

Unlike Euripides, Seneca focuses on the Dionysian and chthonic aspect of Medea and allows no space for ambiguities. His Medea is not simply a paradigmatic practitioner of the occult but an agent of evil. She can be said to be a precursor of today's satanists. There is no rationality in her, no Apollonian temperance and sensibility, no σοφὶα, only mental disturbance.

In Seneca's version there is a significant change in the myth. Medea's exceptional character and personality which in Euripides was associated with witchcraft is developed by Seneca into a mental and existential agitation. The skill of witchcraft is replaced by the innate quality of malice. Evil, which in Euripides is just a potential, realizes itself in Seneca's play. It could be argued that Seneca is challenging (perhaps intentionally) Euripides's play and, in particular, the very nature of the main character.

In Christa Wolf's novel, *Medea,* Medea's sorcery is neither witchcraft nor evil practice but a therapeutic skill. Medea is a healer, a Heilerin: she helps people recover from physical as well as emotional injuries. She is a peaceful person, gifted with understanding, patience and serenity and the ability to heal people's minds and bodies. She is only considered a sorceress by the people of Corinth who are unable to understand her personality and her mentality: "...she soothed me with her words, no, it was more than soothing, it was, one of her sorcerer's tricks, that's clear to me now." (Wolf 1999, 111) Wolf's Medea is a benevolent person who tries to inspire self-respect and self-confidence in the people around her. She practises a remedial kind of sorcery aiming at restoring the mind, body and spirit of the people who seek her help. Her motives are purely altruistic. Unlike the versions of Euripides and Seneca, where Medea's sorcery focuses on Jason, Wolf's Medea uses her skills and gifts to help anybody who is in pain or trouble. Her attempt to help the daughter of the king overcome her fears and her epilepsy is an obvious example of her benevolent nature. The emphasis here is on the spirit.

Medea's intelligence is depicted by Wolf as acute intuition and perception, which enables her to be a healer. It is this perception, this inner vision that signifies her otherness and her outcast status within Corinthian society. Men are scared of her free and lively spirit, and women are jealous of her charming and outstanding personality. While Euripides has Medea simply admitting that she is hated and envied because of her *σοφὶα*, Christa Wolf shows in detail which thoughts, emotions and reactions Medea's personality elicits to other people around her. First and foremost, Jason experiences feelings of frustration towards Medea. His first, immediate reactions upon meeting her in her father's palace in Colchis, are shock and enchantment:

> The way she stood there, stooped over, in that red and white tiered skirt and close-fitting black top they all wear, and caught the water from the spout in her cupped hands and drank. The way she straightened up and noticed us, shook her hands dry, and approached us frankly, taking quick, strong steps, slender, but with a well-developed figure, and showing off all the virtues of her appearance to such advantage that Telamon, with his usual lack of self-control, whistled through his teeth and whispered to me: Now there's something nice for you.
>
> A pulling in all my limbs such as I'd never known, a feeling of absolute enchantment – she's put a spell on me went through my mind, and in fact, so she had. (ibid., 32)

Jason is enthralled not only by Medea's physical attributes but mainly by her natural grace and magnificent aura. In fact, the very first thing that impresses him is the way she moves and performs trivial daily activities, such as drinking water from the fountain, shaking her hands dry, walking and talking. By his own admission it is her dark features that initially attract him but primarily it is her exceptional personality as manifested in her mannerisms and behaviour that captivates him.

Her incisive perception is demonstrated in her attempt to help Jason in Colchis, and her strong will makes him fall in love with her. "My consciousness abandoned me" he admits (ibid., 46). Monika Shafi points out that Medea's willingness to help Jason is not a sign of weakness but a demonstration of her strong personality.

> Ihre Medea ist eine kluge, einfühlsame, stolze und unabhängige Frau, die Kolchis nicht aus blinder Liebe zu Jason verließt, sondern um dem verknöcherten, autoritären und unmenschlichen Regime ihres Vaters Aietes zu entfliehen. (Shafi 1997, 377)
>
> Her Medea is a clever, compassionate, proud and independent woman, who left Kolchis not because of blind love to Jason but to escape the rigid authoritarian and inhuman regime of her father Aietes. (My translation)

Much as he admires her and is attracted to her because of her outstanding, charismatic personality, Jason is also frustrated as he cannot fully comprehend his wife's character. When, for example, Medea refuses to bind her hair like Corinthian women do, Jason perceives that as an act of arrogance and rebellion. He is unable to understand her exuberance which contrasts with the mild and submissive temperament of Corinthian women. "That woman will do me in" (Wolf 1999, 29) he concludes, unable to understand his wife and deal with her.

While to Jason, Medea elicits feelings of attraction and frustration, to other people she evokes the "envy" and "ill-will" mentioned in the Euripidean text. Agameda, Medea's former pupil, is envious of her teacher's unique charisma and tries to distance herself from the influence of Medea's personality.

> There it was again. The intoxication that overcomes me when I'm in Medea's presence overcame me – but for the last time. Now I know I'm safe. Safe from her damned tricks and her famous emanations. (ibid., 54)

Agameda, detests Medea for her "damned tricks" and her "famous emanations" which are nothing but acute perception. One of her so-called tricks, perceived by Corinthians as an exercise of witchcraft, was to help them deal with famine by encouraging them to eat horseflesh and by teaching them to grow edible, wild plants. Instead of gratitude she faces ostracism and is labelled a witch even by Kreon's astronomer, Akamas.

At this point the notions of the consanguinity, metamorphosis and potency of myth and their significance in literature, become more explicit. When Euripides is mentioning the "envy" and "ill-will" that people feel towards Medea, he establishes the link which perpetuates the myth of Medea and operates as one essential element of kinship between the Euripidean play and the novel by Wolf. It is this consanguinity that in turn establishes the metamorphosis of the myth and affirms its vigour.

The fact that Wolf's version is a novel can partly account for the thorough presentation of thoughts and emotions and it can be argued that Wolf deliberately did not write a drama, where the unfolding of the inner world of the characters would be exhausted in lengthy soliloquies. There is, of course, a strong element of drama since the novel is subtitled *Stimmen* (*Voices*) and consists of ten monologues. However, the novel is not based on action or description but is a graphic disclosure of the innermost thoughts and feelings of the heroine as well as of the other characters. As Turner observes, "Wolf's narrative technique allows the priestess to meditate without the accompaniment of the Chorus, to think rather than merely to rail or declaim" (Turner 1999, 205). Medea's monologues are an uninhibited exposition of her thoughts and emotions, in contrast to the regimented, defensive speeches in the tragedies by Euripides and Seneca.

Furthermore, the end of the novel in which the Corinthians stone Medea's children to death, is a clear affirmation of their hatred of Medea. Wolf therefore develops the idea of Medea's exceptional nature and the effects it has on her life. Medea's intuition also helps her discover the reality of Corinth, namely that the civilized city hides great atrocities and macabre secrets. Medea, as Christa Wolf portrays her, is a charismatic woman with the talent to delve into the human psyche and try to bring peace.

A very significant element that Wolf introduces in her version is the fact that Medea's children are stoned to death by the Corinthian people. According to Georgina Paul, Wolf based her version on Robert Graves's account of the story of Medea in which he mentions the scholiast Hyginus, and argues that Medea's children were murdered and Euripides was bribed in order to present Medea as the killer of her own children (Paul 1997, 227-240).

Medea, Stimmen challenges, thus, the original myth by introducing information that has been ignored sheding light on certain ambiguities of the Euripidean text. Euripides does have Medea kill her children and he does refer to her sorcery skills; however the woman he portrays possesses a great degree of rationality and an outstanding personality and mind which is evident in her dialogues with Kreon and Jason. As previously mentioned there is a great degree of vacillation on the part of Euripides regarding the good or evil nature of Medea. Readers have been conditioned to read the Euripidean text as a representation of female madness and emotional disturbance. This has happened because Seneca's version has contributed greatly to the impression that Euripides's Medea is just a lunatic, vindictive female. This reading has not only reduced Medea to a caricature of the enraged, betrayed wife but it has also deprived the Euripidean text of its comprehensive nature. Furthermore, as Angeliki Kottaridou mentions in her essay, "Medea – the price for knowledge", "With the rising influence of rationalism, the image of Medea, whose essence contradicts the prevalent beliefs, acquires more and more darker aspects." (Kottaridou 1995, 25). With Christa Wolf we have not only a new transformation of the myth but also an enlightening and enlightened depiction of Medea, which eventually restores her status in the literary canon and reveals new aspects of the Euripidean play. As Barbara Turner points out:

> The portrait of the lovelost, thus hysterical Medea - a traditional if inexact reading of the Euripidean version - reverts to that of a cunning, perceptive observer, who uncovers Creon's guilt and must therefore be taken out of the way. Indeed, Wolf gives perhaps not a version of the story but a presentation of its structural underpinnings, the causal chains which lead to the currency of Medea's infamy. (Turner 1999, 205)

It can be argued of course that Euripides's play does not qualify for being the original myth on Medea as it does not consider the view that her children were stoned to death by Corinthians. However, his play illustrates the vacillation between a good and a bad Medea and in that sense it is a comprehensive story. Moreover, the story of Medea is neither a saga nor a legend in which historical information would be of extreme importance. The story of Medea is a myth, and myth is neither pure reality, nor pure fiction but a perennial oscillation between the two. Myth may encompass segments of reality (history, society, politics, facts) but it also embraces the realm of the supernatural, the metaphysical and the transcendental. Euripides's play is the original myth on Medea as it demonstrates exactly this oscillation.

Undoubtedly, more light can be shed onto texts if those are seen as a part of a sequential, dynamic process and compared with one another within this process. The algorithmic evolutionary process of the myth allows interesting comparisons to be made and provides new readings of the texts. Christa Wolf herself admits in one of her interviews:

> Many people believe that the less you know the "freer" you are to invent, but that isn't the case. I find the multitude of sources in this prehistoric field especially stimulating, even exciting, instructive, delightful, but it's indicative of the multitude of a story's possible variants.
> (www.randomhouse.com/boldtype/0498/wolf/notebook.html)

Wolf acknowledges the variegated nature of myth and its importance for literature. In fact, she argues that myth encourages creation because of its multiplicity. What she is actually articulating is the notion of input and output, and more specifically, that the quality of the output depends on the quality and multiplicity of the input.

The different accounts of Medea's sorcery reveal how the myth of Medea possesses the potential for evolution and how this potential materializes itself in the case of sorcery. The three different texts illustrate the ramifications of the original myth and its dynamic nature. At this point, Cassirer's concept of metamorphosis assumes a more intelligible form and justifies its introduction and application in the study of myth.[20] The next step is to look at the sequences that result from the three different inputs in the flow chart. First let's look at the feelings that Medea has for Jason which make her attach herself to him and devote her life to him.

In Euripides Medea's love for Jason is a strong, compelling feeling which enables her to commit incredible atrocities. Her heart is "a heart on fire" (Euripides 1958, 39), heart which is totally devoted to Jason and goes to extremes for his sake. Medea herself admits that her love for him surpasses all her other qualities including her intelligence: "And then, showing more willingness to help than wisdom, I killed him, Pelias, with a

---

[20] Cassirer, in fact, contrives the term "law of metamorphosis" which he argues characterizes the mythic world. For Cassirer, the natural and the mythic world share a lot of fundamental principles and are inextricably linked. One of these fundamental principles is the principle of motion and change or what he calls the "unbroken continuous". See Cassirer 1945, 72-107.

most dreadful death at his own daughter's hands, and took away your fear." (ibid., 41) Her devotion to him goes as far as performing murders for him so as to facilitate his project of acquiring the Golden Fleece. Apollonius's version has Hera and Athena making Medea fall in love with Jason blindly (albeit with the help of Eros), and consequently leaving her at the mercy of her infatuation.[21] Euripides though, creates a heroine who is not a toy, an ἄθυρμα, in the hands of the Olympians, but an exceptional and charismatic woman who possesses strong will, a sharp mind as well as emotional strength and therefore feels, thinks and acts by herself. He creates a female character who is beyond the average, a woman who can reach what is beyond the real, the tangible and the ordinary. H.D.F. Kitto (1993, 190-192) mentions that we cannot identify with Medea and feel the Aristotelian pity and fear, because Medea is an extraordinary character, not in terms of status (such as Oedipus for example) but in terms of compound. It is only natural therefore that Medea will experience great passion and intense feelings for Jason and will deviate from the usual manner in which a woman relates to a man.[22] In her response to Kreon, she admits her own awareness of the fact that she is above the average person. Medea's immediate reaction after Jason's marriage to Kreon's daughter is withdrawal and depression. "She lies without food and gives herself up to suffering, wasting away every moment of the day in tears." (Euripides 1958, 26) She laments for her life which she now considers wretched since she has lost the object of her worship and devotion. Yet, there is an insinuation that she will not be content with mourning, but that she is likely to attempt an active exhibition of her devastation and betrayal. "I am afraid she may think of some dreadful thing, for her heart is violent." (ibid., 27) Her nurse, who knows her very well is aware that her wounded pride will seek justice. It is important though to remember that Euripides provides a well-organised version of Medea's personality and justifies in that way the seminal nature of the play.

This passion leads her to revenge, and it is this passion that Seneca uses as a basic ingredient and builds upon by taking it to its extreme version, that of obsession and hysteria. This is yet another demonstration of the idea of consanguinity which can be seen in the passion of Medea for Jason, which Euripides simply refers to, but Seneca bases his tragedy on.

In Seneca, Medea's love for Jason is not the typical passionate love of a woman who dedicates her life and existence to a man. Seneca presents us with a woman whose love is abnormal, diseased and therefore dangerous.

---

[21] See Apollonius Rhodius 1912, 203-205 and 245-251.

[22] According to D.L. Page, (1988, xiv) "Here, indeed, for the first time in the Greek theatre, the power of the drama lies rather in the characters than in their actions. Medea's emotions are far more moving than her revenge."

"Murder and impious bloodshed how often have I wrought! – and yet no crime have I done in wrath; 'twas ill-omened love that stirred me." (Seneca 1960, 239) This idea of the "ill-omened love" enhances the notion of the mental disturbance of Medea. Even her feelings of love and devotion are contaminated with sickness and distortion. Medea is obsessed with Jason, and once she loses him she becomes mad. In her last attempt to change his mind, suggesting to him to flee with her and he refuses, she receives a great shock. "He has gone! Can it be so? Goest thou, forgetful of me and all the deeds I wrought?" (ibid., 279) Earlier, during her conversation with Jason, she points out the deeds and crimes she has committed in order to help him. "For thee my country has given place, for thee father, brother, maidenhood." (ibid., 269). Medea has been, in fact, protecting and helping Jason in order to secure her position next to him. It was not genuine love and sacrificial nature that inspired and motivated her to commit all these atrocities so as to promote and protect Jason's position. Her ostensible sacrifices were, in fact, acts of cunning with an ulterior motive, namely, to reinforce Jason's dependence upon and commitment to her. She therefore holds him responsible too for the murders she has committed.

It is because of Seneca's version that Medea has been closely associated and often identified with madness and mental disturbance. In Euripides, Medea is passionate but still sane, which adds to the dramatic stature of her character. Furthermore, she possesses an acute mind which she makes use of. In Seneca, however, Medea's mental state is characterized by confusion and disruption. Although still capable of some basic reasoning and argumentation, she is overwhelmed by hysteria and malevolence. It is not simply an excess of emotions and a violation of the Aristotelian virtue which, according to Martha Nussbaum (1997, 219-229), is the reason for Medea's vindictive mood. Nussbaum does have a point in relating Medea to passionate and excessive love. However, it is not in Seneca's Medea that this point finds application and justification but in Euripides's Medea. Nussbaum's discussion pertains to a healthy individual who was somehow caught up in an erotic frenzy and lost control of her thoughts, feelings and actions. This discussion is complemented by Ruth Padel's investigation of madness in Classical Greece, according to which anybody was a potential victim of a madness attack – which was a temporary condition – and we have a Medea as Nussbaum describes her.[23]

[23] Ruth Padel (1995) explains that in Classical Greece madness was considered a temporary state. Even in cases where there was a susceptibility towards mental disturbance, the permanence pertained to the susceptibility itself, whereas the disturbance was temporary: it was a fit or an attack. The word oistros suggests such an attack of an erotic, procreative nature. See Ruth Padel, Chapters 2 and 4.

However, such a Medea is hardly Seneca's heroine. His Medea is a seriously disturbed individual, with very few signs of mental health. This does not of course debase the significance and the literary merits of the play but it confirms the role of the play in an algorithmic sequence. The mere consideration of the play as a part of this process illustrates its particular quality while asserting the metamorphosis of the myth. In fact, it is due to this kind of kinship between the Euripidean and the Senecan version that the two texts have often been confused.

In Seneca's tragedy Medea is associated with evil and, consequently, her feelings for Jason are of an evil, dark and malicious nature.

The point of culmination is the state of hysteria that overwhelms her as a result of Jason's betrayal. Unlike the Euripidean Medea, who mourns and falls into depression, Seneca's Medea is caught up in a manic state. Her nurse describes the symptoms of her hysteria:

> As a Meanad uncertainly directs her frenzied steps when now she raves at the oncoming of the god, on snowy Pindus' top or on Nysa's ridges, so she runs now here, now there, with frantic rush, marks of distracted passion in her face. Her cheeks aflame, she pants with deep sobs for breath, shouts aloud weeps floods of tears, beams with joy; she assumes the proof of every passion Whither the weight of her wrath inclines, where it aims its threats, hangs still in doubt; she threatens, seethes with rage, complains, groans aloud. Where will this wave break itself? Madness o'erflowd its bounds. No simple or half-way crime doth she ponder in her heart; she will outdo herself. I recognise the marks of her old-time rage. (Seneca 1960, 261)

Medea herself admits that she is insane "... my madness shall never cease its quest of vengeance and shall grow on for ever." (ibid., 263) "Perplexed, witless, with mind scarce sane, I am tossed to every side." (ibid., 273) Medea's association with hysteria has led a lot of people to conclude that she is actually a hysterical woman in the clinical sense of the word.

Harold Loomis Cleasby maintains that Seneca's rendition of Medea as an evil and mentally disturbed person is a result of his highly rhetorical style which is in accordance with the dramatic conventions of Roman times. For Cleasby, it is this preoccupation with rhetoric that accounts for the one-dimensional character of Seneca's Medea.

> We must not expect a careful psychology in Seneca's delineation of the human emotions; occasionally his personages seem to be little more than convenient mouthpieces for exercises in rhetorical declamation. In the *Medea* he has attained a measure of success in character-drawing that he has not reached in many of his other plays, but even here the workmanship is rough, and the coloring, although brilliant, is crude and monotonous. (Cleasby 1907, 65)

In Christa Wolf's novel, Medea's love for Jason is a serene yet strong love which involves lust as well as emotions. Her passion for him is quiet and transcends the typical passion that a woman can feel for a man. She loves Jason in a calm, patient way but also feels a strong attraction to him.

Finally, her reaction is neither anger, nor hysteria but a dignified disappointment. She feels victimized since her children are murdered. However she departs for exile in a quiet way. Contrary to the other versions, here Medea is the object of vindication and anger. She is a Christ-like figure who is victimized, and peacefully accepts the penalty.

> As silent as I was when they came and put me under arrest. They charged me with having led the women who committed violence upon Turon. I made no reply. Everything was proceeding according to a plan over which I no longer had any influence. Early this morning they came and fetched me. For the trial, they said, and brought me here to this tiny dark room. (Wolf 1999, 161)

In Euripides the result of Medea's passion is revenge, which is achieved through the killing of the two children. Revenge is the result of betrayal and the reaction to feelings of disappointment, injustice and deprivation. It is not the product of an evil nature but, on the contrary, it is the reaction of an impassioned woman who invested her whole life in a man. The atrocity involved in this revenge is attributed by Medea herself, to her feminine cunning, employed to provide the best revenge for Jason. "Ah, Medea, in your plotting and scheming leave nothing untried of all those things which you know. You have the skill. What is more you were born a woman, and women, though most helpless in doing good deeds, are of every evil the cleverest of contrivers." (Euripides 1958, 38-39)

Euripides provides us with the process: witchcraft-passion-revenge.

In Seneca, Medea wishes to bring destruction and this is part of her maliciousness. Upon hearing of Jason's marriage to the daughter of Kreon, "Already borne, borne is my vengeance!" (Seneca 1960, 231), she doesn't want simply to revenge but to bring catastrophe and misfortune. "The only calm for me – if with me I see the universe overwhelmed in ruins; with me let all things pass away. 'Tis sweet to drag others down when thou art perishing" (ibid., 265). The process here is: evil-obsession-destruction.

Finally, in Christa Wolf's version, the conclusion is a peaceful one with Medea being the victim of hatred and conspiracy. There is no tension, and even the stoning of her children is mentioned by Medea in a manner that is deprived of any animosity. The ending is consistent with Medea's quality as a healer and the final stage of the process: healing-love-peace.

Based on the preceding discussion, the fundamental myth of Medea is that of an exceptional and charismatic woman, inclined to strong passions and capable of creation as well as destruction.

The three versions of Medea demonstrate the metamorphosis that the myth can undergo when some of its elements are changed. In fact, the algorithmic reading of the texts demonstrates that they actually belong to a wider process of evolution of the myth of Medea. This idea, I believe, enables us to look at the texts in a wider context and understand them, not simply as individual works or as works representative of an era, but as vital and living parts of a continuous flow.

This Chapter has shown how the potency of myth can assist comparative literary analysis (although it can in no way be seen as a panacea in the realm of literary discussion), and thus qualify myth as a legitimate approach to literary texts. More particularly, I examined mythic metamorphosis and the distillation of a fundamental myth out of a comparative analysis of different versions of that myth.

In the following chapters I shall illustrate how the process of distillation of a fundamental myth can be used as a tool for literary analysis of primary texts. In the final chapter I shall discuss an already distilled fundamental myth (Robert Graves's White Goddess as the fundamental myth on female liminality), and its use in literary discussion.

CHAPTER TWO

DEMYTHOLOGIZING *YERMA*: THE STRUGGLE BETWEEN PROCREATION AND RECREATION AND THE FALLACY OF MOTHERHOOD

Federico García Lorca's tragedy *Yerma* has been classified as a play about motherhood and the idea of procreation. Yerma as a character is considered the epitome of the childless, and thus frustrated, woman and a symbol for the perennial question of sterility. The heroine was perceived by critics of the time as "a pathological case, with a one track mind, obsessive, crazy,"[24] "a victim of an obsession"[25] and her ardent desire for a child was seen as "an evident manifestation of paranoia."[26] The play was received with rather disapproving and highly judgmental comments such as the one found in the *Diario de Madrid* in 1934 which saw in *Yerma* an exaggeration of the theme of sterility as an attempt on the part of Lorca to elevate it to the level of tragedy.[27]

The play is an explicit exposition of the strong desire for motherhood and procreation. However, there are latent and particular references in the text which indicate that the essence of Yerma's tragedy is neither motherhood nor procreation as such, but her profound desire for sexual and emotional fulfilment in her marriage. The concept of motherhood is the solid stratum for the dramatic construction of the play and it is undoubtedly the most significant and legitimate theme of the play. Nonetheless, the discussion and analysis of the theme of motherhood and procreative frustration, apart from its relatively easy exhaustion, operates as a restrictive factor for the character of Yerma by reducing her to a caricature of the childless, semi-hysterical, neurotic woman. Furthermore, it constitutes a

[24] This review comes from the newspaper *La Epoca* and was written after the premiere of the play in Madrid in December 1934 (Tubert 1993, 70).
[25] See Fernández-Cifuentes 1984, 288.
[26] This review comes from the newspaper *El Correo Catalan* and it followed the premiere of the play in Barcelona in September 1935 (ibid.).
[27] See Tubert 1993, 71.

deviation from (or in fact a misinterpretation of) the vital and sine qua non theme of the play: the quest for sexual marital fulfilment. In other words, *Yerma* is not and cannot be exhausted in elaborate analyses on the childless mother and her frustrations. Neither can it be restricted to the literary and philosophical analyses of the concept of sterility. This Chapter argues that Yerma's tragedy is her lack of a sexually and emotionally fulfilling relationship with her husband, and that her obsessive yearning for a child is nothing but a disguise for her profound desire for such a relationship. Her persistence and obstinancy over motherhood as a panacea for her desolate state and her unhappiness in her marriage reveals a fallacious apprehension of motherhood which, for Yerma, is an alibi for her sexual and emotional marital void. In order to illustrate my argument, I shall explore notions of motherhood as rendered in three versions of the myth of Demeter. Out of this analysis I shall distil a comprehensive notion of the Demetrian motherhood, which I see as fallacious, and finally I shall show how this fallacious motherhood applies to Yerma and the implications it has for the interpretation of the play.[28] More particularly, I shall question the nature of Demeter's maternal feelings and discuss the notion of motherhood presented in the three versions, as a state of dependence and frustration. At the same time, I shall question the nature of Yerma's desire for motherhood and discuss her character and her persistence over motherhood in the light of Demetrian motherhood in order to reveal her true tragedy which is her own lack of sexual marital fulfilment.

The three main texts under consideration with respect to the myth of Demeter are the "Homeric hymn to Demeter", Alfred Lord Tennyson's poem "Demeter and Persephone" and Rita Dove's collection of poems titled

---

[28] A legitimate and inevitable objection to the choice of the figure of Demeter is the argument that there is no ostensible relation between Demeter and Yerma's quest for sexual fulfilment, since Demeter is not usually associated with sexuality and eroticism. Indeed, in terms of sexuality Aphrodite seems to be the most appropriate mythological figure for the discussion of Yerma. Nonetheless, the significance of the employment and application of mythological figures in literary analysis is not exhausted in the location and discussion of qualitative, thematic, narrative, archetypal and/or semantic similarities, but it expands to the comparative discussion of seemingly unrelated figures, elements or texts, and the eventual interpretative and illuminating effect of the mythic source on the text under analysis. See also Chapter 1, "The Dynamics of Myth". In the case of Demeter and Yerma it is particularly challenging to look at Demetrian motherhood as a rather problematic state of possession and as a disguise for various emotional needs. Yerma's obsession with motherhood becomes less incomprehensible when discussed in the light of Demetrian motherhood, and furthermore, the whole play in its entirety seen in a new light.

Mother Love. The Homeric hymn constitutes the original myth concerning Demeter, since it is a complete and organized account of the story of the goddess, as opposed to many other fragmentary and incomplete, though equally interesting, sources from antiquity.[29] Tennyson's poem and Dove's collection are the transformed versions of the original myth.

All three texts share a fundamental understanding of motherhood as a state of dependence on the part of the mother, and progressively they depict the mother's own sense of being incapable of living without her daughter. Each of the works adopts its own perspective and illustrates a different aspect of an erroneous notion of motherhood by portraying the emotional and mental experience of a mother without her child and the implications of this experience on the mother herself. The ancient Greek text is a rather rigid and gloomy narration of the abduction of Persephone and her mother's desperation upon realizing the loss, while the Victorian poem is a dramatic monologue of Demeter who recalls the sorrow she experienced while without her daughter and revives her hope at the prospect of Persephone's annual visits on earth. Finally, the poems by Dove provide a psychological insight to the myth and introduce very interesting questions with respect to the connotation and the implications of Demetrian motherhood for the mother as well as the daughter by focusing on the relationship between the two women and more particularly on its process of development and its implications for both parties.

I would like to suggest the following flow chart with respect to the transformations of the myth of Demeter.

[29] See Chapter 1, "The Dynamics of Myth", Blumenberg's distinction between *original* and *fundamental* myth.

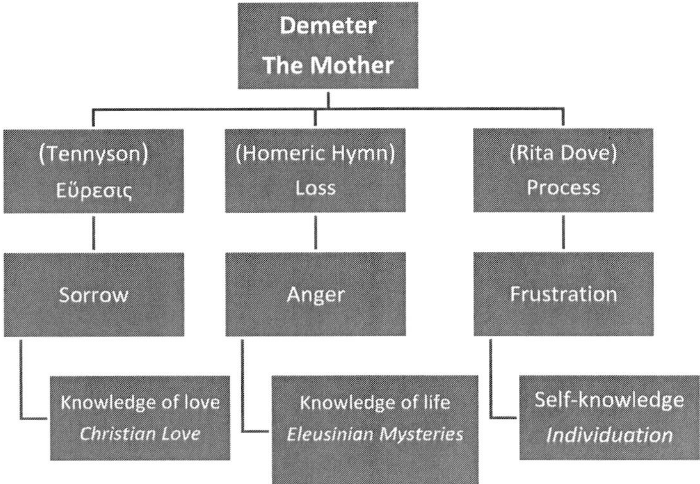

While the notion of motherhood is the common denominator of the three versions and affirms Cassirer's concept of consanguinity in mythic transformation, the variants in each version constitute the transformative catalysts that produce the particular metamorphoses of the Demeter myth.

An important differentiation therefore is the choice of emphasis on the part of each poet. While Tennyson's emphasis is on the reunion of the mother and the daughter or else the *εὕρεσις* of the daughter, which reverses the emphasis on the loss of the daughter of the Homeric hymn, Dove adopts a modernist perspective and concentrates on the psychological processes involved in a mother-daughter relationship, while exploring its dynamics.

The "Homeric hymn to Demeter" is a graphic account of the origins of the Eleusinian mysteries. The title presupposes Demeter as the theme and focus of the narrative which indeed she is. "Thick-haired Demeter, dread goddess, I sing to begin" (Sargent 1975, 2)/"Δήμητρ' ἠΰκομον σεμνὴν θεὰν ἄρχομ' ἀείδειν." (Papaditsas and Ladia 1997, 12) These are the very first words of the hymn which function as an introduction to the text. Nonetheless, the text immediately indicates that although Demeter is its manifest object, it is only through her daughter, Persephone, that she becomes the focus of the hymn: "Her and her slim-ankled daughter, whom Hades abducted, granted the right by far-seeing Zeus of loud thunder." (Sargent 1975, 2) The entire hymn, in fact, focuses on the reactions of Demeter after she has found out that her daughter has been abducted. While the title is suggestive of a praise of a distinctive deity – a goddess who is σεμνὴ, graceful and worthy of respect and reverence, and a very significant goddess indeed by virtue of her power over harvest, agriculture and vegetation in general – it is early on made obvious that she is referred to in conjunction with her daughter and moreover she is defined through her, and the adventure of her abduction. The word hymn itself suggests high praise, which in the case of Demeter is exhausted in and restricted to specific adjectives: ἠΰκομος, σεμνὴ, ποτνία, ἄνασσα, καλλιστέφανος, τιμάοχος. The narrative often operates in a reductive way with respect to Demeter, particularly where her reactions and emotions over Persephone's abduction are concerned: the goddess is portrayed as a mother whose anger and rage prevail over her sadness and grief. In short, the Homeric hymn is exhausted in the narration of Persephone's abduction and the reactions of Demeter, raising thereby, legitimate questions about the nature and thematic objective of the hymn, as well as the stature of the goddess.

It is interesting here to note that although, as the goddess of harvest and agriculture, Demeter could be very well identified with Mother Earth or the mother of all living things, still nowhere in the hymn do we find such a reference to her. Nowhere do we see Demeter symbolizing a wider notion of motherhood and representing qualities such as self-renunciation, sacrifice, creation, generosity, support, qualities which are inextricably linked with motherhood. In fact the role of the Mother Earth is given to Gaia, justifying thus Gaia's participation in the project of Persephone's abduction.[30] Neither are there any references to Demeter as the corn goddess (which is her definitive quality within the realm of the Olympians) apart from the destruction of the crops which constitutes her revenge on the Olympians. The absence of such references in the original myth of Demeter, while fostering her establishment as the goddess of motherhood, raises some interesting issues such as the association of an aetiological myth about the vegetation cycle and the establishment of the Eleusinian mysteries with Demeter the mother and not with Demeter the goddess of grain, agriculture and fertility.

---

[30] Gaia as Mother Earth has no reason to object to Persephone's marriage to Hades. On the contrary, she supports a fusion of the chthonic and the earthly world since her domain encompasses the whole of creation. She therefore facilitates the seduction of Persephone by presenting her with a narcissus flower as a bait. In the 'Homeric hymn to Gaia' she is referred to as the Mother of all, παμμήτηρα and μήτηρα πὰντων and as the eldest of all beings, πρεσβίστην. I believe that Gaia corresponds to the conceptual and metaphysical dimension of motherhood as opposed to Demeter who represents the psychological aspect; however progressively an identification of the two occurred and therefore Demeter acquired a wider range of qualities.

In other words, in the Homeric hymn, the goddess's status is reduced to the emotional experiences of a mother who loses her daughter and more particularly the reactions of grief, but mostly anger and bitterness that she exhibits. Eventually, as this Chapter shall illustrate, the hymn, which sets out to praise the goddess, becomes an indictment.

The Homeric hymn opens with an immediate reference to Persephone's abduction which is the main theme: "Thick-haired Demeter, dread goddess, I sing to begin, her and her slim-ankled daughter, whom Hades abducted, granted the right by far-seeing Zeus of loud thunder." (Sargent 1975, 2) In the original, verb ἥρπαξεν (abducted) which actually means snatched/seized, suggests not only the violent nature of the act but also the sense of deprivation and loss. Indeed, the narration that follows is a chronicle of the loss of Persephone as this is experienced by her mother. The Hymn tells us of the actual event of the abduction and of Demeter's reactions: her anger and grief, her descent in disguise to the world of mortals and her attempt to nurse Demophoon, her subsequent revenge on the Olympians through the destruction of the crops and, finally, her joy upon reunion with Persephone. The emphasis on the bereavement that Demeter experiences becomes more pronounced through the gloomy and joyless atmosphere; the heart of Demeter "overflowing with sorrow", her depressed state where "in her grief [she] touched neither ambrosia nor nectar", her choice of disguise as an old woman sitting in a shady spot, her "silently grieving" attitude while at Metaneira's house are but an indication of the prevalent sombre mood. Carl Kerenyi points out that the Homeric hymn in its entirety is actually permeated by a gloomy and distressing mood:

> The poet describes Persephone's rape at the beginning of the poem, and from then on it's full of her divine mother's pain and grief. Even in their reunion there is still a portion of bitterness, for Persephone has eaten, while with her husband, of the pomegranate and has to spend a third of every year with him. (Jung and Kerenyi 1970, 158)

Indeed, the emphasis of the hymn continues to be on the loss, even at the end, when finally, there is a reunion and Demeter knows that Persephone will spend most of the year with her. Even when the goddess finally meets Persephone, she is not overwhelmed by joy or happiness, but rushes to reunite with her daughter; "just as a maenad, frenzied, rushes down the forested mountain" (Sargent 1975, 11). The metaphor of the frenzied maenad, clearly renders Demeter's obsession with her daughter and her almost hysterical state upon seeing her, but most significantly it suggests the feelings of distress and frustration that the goddess experiences, even at the moment of her reunion with her daughter. This distress is very well reflected in the way she welcomes Persephone.

> But while yet enfolding her child in her arms, Demeter,
> Her mind at once suspicious of treachery, violently trembled,
> And left off caressing her daughter and straightway addressed her:
> "Tell me, my child, did you eat any food at all down below?
> Speak out, and hide nothing from me, that we may both know.
> For if not, you are free of the loathsome dominion of Hades,
> And may dwell with me and your father, cloud-wrapped son of Cronos, Held
> in honor by all of the immortal gods everlasting.
> But if you have eaten, back you must go to the depths of the earth,
> There to live for a third of the span of each year,
> But the other two seasons with me and the other immortals.
> But when the earth blooms with all kinds of sweet-smelling flowers
> In springtime, you will come up again from the kingdom
> Of shadows – a wonder indeed for gods and for mortal mankind.
> But tell me how he carried you off to his shadowy kingdom,
> The ruthless receiver of many. What bait did he use to ensnare you?"
>
> (ibid., 12)

Demeter is unable to enjoy the meeting itself and the embrace of her daughter. Her "suspicious" and restless mind seeks to ensure the permanence of Persephone's presence next to her mother. The momentary pleasure deriving from the embrace of her daughter – which occurs on Persephone's own initiative: "And at the sight of the lovely face of her mother, Persephone, leaping down from the chariot, eagerly ran and threw her arms around her neck and embraced her" (Sargent 1975, 11-12) – is violently interrupted by the thought that Persephone might have eaten the pomegranate seed and therefore will have to spend one third of the year away from her mother. It is very important to clarify the fact that Demeter's anxiety does not concern a permanent absence of Persephone but her annual visit to Hades as the Queen of the Underworld, and therefore Demeter's apprehension is exaggerated. It is only Persephone who exhibits a purely emotional and spontaneous reaction upon seeing her mother "leaping down from the chariot", running towards her and embracing her (ibid., 1-12), adding thus a joyous and merry mood to the so far dreary hymn. Demeter's "frenzied" state while away from Persephone, and her obsessive desire to have her by her side, constantly indicate an overprotective and problematic relationship on the part of the mother.

Tennyson's poem is titled "Demeter and Persephone", which again implies the definition and perception of the goddess through her daughter.

However, the title clarifies and establishes the idea that the poem is about Demeter and her daughter, while revealing the deliberate intention of the poet to isolate a specific aspect of the myth and dwell on it. The poem is a dramatic monologue of Demeter, a fact which automatically suggests that it reflects her own perspective and does not claim either to glorify or even simply describe her. In her book *Alfred Tennyson* Elaine Jordan (1988, 82) points out that, "the monologues are metaphors for states of mind, divided between rest and motion, soliloquy and narrative, metaphor and metonymy." Indeed, Demeter's monologue is a rendition of her own state of mind and illustrates her point of view while revealing the emotional repercussions of Persephone's abduction on her. In other words, the poem is an attempted disclosure of the inner feelings, moods and psychological disposition of the mythological goddess in relation to a particular incident hence the title "Demeter and Persephone" which leaves no misconception regarding the focal point of the poem.

The relationship between mother and daughter is presented through subjectivity, and it begins with εὕρεσις after Persephone has spent some time in the Underworld and finally ascends to the realm of mortals to see her mother, initiating thus her annual journeys to Hades. The Tennysonian Demeter refers to her dark days during Persephone's absence in retrospect when finally the two women meet and reunite demonstrating a more optimistic perspective than the one in the Homeric hymn; however, the relationship between Demeter and Persephone is restricted to the former's sorrow and search for her daughter while the significance of εὕρεσις for both mother and daughter seems to be rather undermined via the narration of Demeter's account of the abduction.

The overall emphasis however seems to be on the reunion, the εὕρεσις which in the Homeric hymn is the last part of the narrative. Tennyson reverses the order of the original myth by placing the εὕρεσις in the beginning of his poem and by providing the subtitle "In Enna". Enna, apart from being the location of Demeter's palace, is also the location of Persephone's abduction as well as of the eventual reunion of mother and daughter and as such it signifies the completion of an adventure and the commencement of a new stage in the relationship between the two. Moreover, it indicates Tennyson's will to depart from the pessimism of the original version and appropriate the myth to a modern, christianized optimism. The diction and imagery of the first part of the poem suggest explicitly the prevalent joyous mood and the optimistic predisposition of the poet himself towards his theme. The image of the nightingale who, upon seeing Persephone, "flash'd into a frolic of song and welcome" (Tennyson 1892, 15) proclaims the merriment and excitement of Demeter and also enhances the idea of a macrocosmic participation in this mirth. This atmosphere of joy becomes even more pronounced when juxtaposed to the cold and unfeeling atmosphere of the Homeric hymn and the depiction of the meeting of the two women. While in the Homeric hymn the moment of reunion is shadowed by the distress of Demeter caused by her suspicion that Persephone might have eaten the pomegranate seed, in "Demeter and Persephone" the joy of εὕρεσις is magnified through the presence of the sun who "burst from a swimming fleece of winter gray, and robed thee in his day from head to feet" (ibid.) and the appreciation of the very moment of reunion:

> So in this pleasant vale we stand again,
> The field of Enna, now once more ablaze
> with flowers that brighten as thy footstep falls.
>
> (ibid., 16)

Tennyson himself was aware of the alterations in the myth that his version signified. He consciously refrained from simply retelling the story of Demeter and Persephone and chose to provide a new way of looking at an old myth. When his son Hallam suggested to him to write a poem about the old story of Demeter and Persephone, Tennyson replied: "I will write it, but when I write an antique like this I must put it into a frame – something modern about it. It is no use giving a mere *rechauffé* of old legends." (Tennyson Hallam 1897, 364) The poet, obviously aware of the dangers that the reworking of an old story involves, was cautious not simply to rekindle an ancient myth but to transform it and adapt it to a more contemporary context.[31] He therefore provides a truly new version of the myth by positioning the notion of the annulment of death through resurrection within the Christian ideology. Most critics including Ricks and Jordan consent to the Christian connotative frame of the poem, which for them is manifested not only in the notion of death and resurrection, but in the sacrificial role of Persephone, who assumes a role similar to that of Christ.[32] The merriment

[31] Curtis Dahl (1958, 356-362) offers an interesting discussion of what Tennyson might have meant by more than a *rechauffé*; he argues that Tennyson's modern frame of the myth of Demeter has two levels: the general level where the poet attempted to adapt an old myth to the contemporary Victorian and Christian ideology and the specific/personal level where Tennyson was responding to Swinburne's materialism and pessimism with a work about the love of God and the belief in immortality.

[32] See Jordan (1988, 81-82) and Ricks (1972, 290).

that characterizes the moment of εὕρεσις resonates with the spirit of joy that is associated with the resurrection of Christ.

The notion of a christianized transformation of the myth complements and justifies the idea of a more optimistic and affirmative tone compared to the ancient hymn and furthermore, it justifies the transformation of latent elements in the original myth.[33]

Interestingly enough, Dove adopts a wider perspective and illustrates the notion of Demetrian motherhood, as perceived by both parties involved, by rendering the inner, emotional state of both the mother and the daughter.[34] The title of her collection is *Mother Love* suggesting the theme and notion of motherhood as such, and not necessarily personal sentiments and emotional reactions. This rather conceptual approach allows for a more conspicuous rendition of Demetrian motherhood since the focus is not so much on the mother, but on the feeling of love as perceived and experienced by the mother as well as the daughter, with some additional insight from third parties. The collection is a mosaic of voices recounting various situations, eventually composing the picture of Demetrian mother love as a fallacious concept which becomes an alibi and an impediment towards self-knowledge and individuation.

The very first poem "Heroes" introduces the main underlying idea of the whole collection, which is "the theme of fragmentation, loss, and regeneration." (Lofgren 1996, 141) The journey towards individuation necessitates a painful and often violent separation, a dramatic schism from the past, but it also results in the achievement of a new independent self. The myth of Demeter is indeed about this process of fragmentation, loss and

---

[33] The concept of alteration of mythic elements and the transformative quality of myth have already been discussed in Chapter 1, where I introduce and discuss the idea of vigour in myth and how this is manifested in a comparative analysis of different texts written on the same myth. Tennyson's distinction between a mere *rechauffé* and a new version of a myth enhances and illustrates well the notion of mythic transformation.

[34] Rita Dove's work is generally characterized by a strong social and racial context. However, in this particular collection of poems the social references serve as an enhancement of the ideas inherent in the poems. Furthermore, as Dove herself points out, even in the case of a strong social framework, this is only because this relates to certain aspects of humanity that she wants to discuss. "I am concerned with race, but certainly not every poem of mine mentions the fact of being black. They are poems about humanity and sometimes humanity happens to be black. I cannot run from, I won't run from any kind of truth." See John Heinz "Rita Dove receives the Heinz Award in the Arts and Humanities for her success in breathing new life into the essence of poetry." http:// www.heinzawards.net/recipients/rita-dove (accessed November 03, 2014).

regeneration not only on Persephone's part but also on Demeter's part. It is not only Persephone who must detach herself from her mother and acquire knowledge of life and of herself; it is also Demeter, or rather the possessive mother, who is in need of a disengagement from her child and of the subsequent experience of loss so that she can achieve individuation and experience a healthier and emotionally balanced motherhood. The beginning of the poem corresponds to the beginning of the ancient hymn, and in particular to the scene where Persephone plucks the narcissus flower because "a marvel to see was this plant for all gods and mortals" (Sargent 1975, 2). Dove, though, converts this mythical incident into a trivial, contemporary scene of a girl picking up a flower from a field in order to capture its beauty before it dies.

> A flower in a weedy field:
> make it a poppy. You pick
> it. Because it begins to wilt
>
> You run to the nearest house
> to ask for a jar of water
>
> (Dove 1995, 3)

In the Homeric hymn the scene of the picking of the narcissus serves a dual purpose: to facilitate the act of the abduction of Persephone by Hades, as well as to join conceptually the story of the abduction and a deeper significance of the myth, which is the notion of earthly fertility and reproduction. In this poem though, the picking of the flower signifies the inevitable severance from the roots, while the subsequent survival of the flower in the jar signifies the regeneration that follows severance; "Significantly, the collection's first image of fragmentation is one of purposeful breaking...A breaking apart is an essential first step toward true self-knowledge and autonomy, for the daughter and even for the mother." (Lofgren 1996, 140)[35] The necessity and the fatality of this "breaking apart" is enhanced through an image of natural determinism: "because it begins to wilt". This teleological contextualization of the original story amalgamates the traditional vegetational theme and the modern psychological interpretation, and cements Dove's transformation of the myth.

The narrator as well as the protagonist in this poem are unidentified so that there is an obscurity as to whom the theme of fragmentation applies.

---

[35] The concept of fragmentation as a prerequisite for maturity in the mother and daughter relationship is, according to Lotta Lofgren, the most important element in Dove's book. See Lofgren 1996, 135-142.

There is no doubt that Dove provides a revitalized and comprehensive version of the original myth of Demeter and achieves a remarkable transformation of it. By introducing the element of self-knowledge and the process towards individuation, she succeeds in re-creating an old myth in a modern context. In fact, she manages to "discover the vibrancy and relevance of myth in acknowledging experience." (Glover 1996, 81)

Dove clearly places the emphasis of the relationship between the mother and the daughter on the process of its evolution. In other words, she portrays the psychological implications of the different stages of this relationship. She presents the process of detachment of the daughter from the mother or, in Lofgren's terms, the fragmentation and the adventurous but also instructive journey towards independence and autonomy. Indicative of this are the titles of some of the poems in the order they are found in the collection: "Primer", "Persephone, Falling", "The Search", "Protection", "The Narcissus Flower", "Persephone Abducted", "Grief: The Council", "Mother Love", "Persephone in Hell", "Hades' Pitch", "Blue Days", "Demeter Mourning", "Demeter, Waiting", "Demeter's Prayers to Hades", "Her island". Alison Booth (1996, 128) adds that, "most scenes are liminal, between places: en route to school, in a garden, down a corridor, in a street, in a car, on tour."[36] This fragmentary representation of the Demeter-Persephone relationship is suggestive of its stages. "Primer", the opening poem the second book of the collection, introduces the story of Demeter and Persephone through the monologue of Persephone. In this disclosure of Persephone's thoughts and feelings we are introduced to her own perception of herself in relation to her mother and her peer group. Persephone in Dove's version is harassed by other girls in her class and, because of her small size, she feels threatened. She manages to escape, though, as her mother comes to rescue her:

> …I survived
> their shoves across the schoolyard
> because my five-foot-zero mother drove up
> in her Caddie to shake them down to size.
>
> (Dove 1995, 7)

The relationship with her mother is based on necessity and dependence on Persephone's part, and over-protection on her mother's part. This aspect of their relationship is not found in the Homeric hymn or "Demeter and

---

[36] Alison Booth (1996, 125-130) dwells on the various facets of multiplicity which permeates *Mother Love* such as multiplicity of voices, languages, images, locations.

Persephone" and it provides a psychological and indeed pragmatic insight into the manner in which the two women are related to each other.

Nonetheless, the wish of the young girl to manage to stand on her own feet and to emancipate herself from her protective mother, is immediately conveyed.

> Nothing could get me into that car.
> I took the long way home, swore
> I'd show them all: I would grow up
>
> (ibid.)

Irrespective of the legitimacy of her mother's concern and act of protection, Persephone feels undermined and underestimated and desires to "grow up". Her choice to walk "the long way home" and her firm refusal to get into her mother's car, clearly indicate her ardent desire to emancipate herself from her mother. The choice of the "long way home" represents her choice of the long journey towards maturity and self-knowledge, which to her is her true "home". The last part of the poem, encapsulates the most significant aspect of Persephone's self-perception and her relationship with her mother and introduces a new dimension to the myth. This trivialization of the classical myth and its protagonists constitutes a major deviation from the original version and, along with the appropriation to a modern context, form the framework of the mythic transformation.

The presence of Persephone's point of view, as well as of the other characters/voices that appear occasionally throughout the collection, provides a variety of perspectives or voices, which not only enrich the work itself but also signify the transformation of the classical myth of Demeter into a twentieth-century myth. The emphasis on individual perceptions, and the fragmentary representation of different voices, point towards a post-Enlightenment, post-modern myth.

In book three, titled "Persephone in Hell", Persephone gives an account of her emotional separation from her mother. The modern American Persephone finds herself in Paris, "girded, then, with youth and good tennis shoes" (Dove 1995, 23) carrying with her the curiosity of her twenty years and the feeling of shelter that her home (America/her mother) has provided her with. By her own admission, she always wanted to "grow-up" and manage to survive without the protective shield that her mother had been providing for her. She therefore allows herself to be lured by new and different experiences, symbolized in French pastries, which become for her the emblems of the seductive power of the unknown.

and at last, squadrons of baked goods:
croissants glazed in the sheen of desire,
the sweating dark caps of the *têtes au negres,*
nipples gleaming on the innocent *beignets;*

(ibid.)

The sexually related diction – desire, sweating, nipples – clearly suggests the seductive power of the Underworld/Paris/the Unknown, debunking therefore the notion of the violent and brutal abduction and rape – ἥρπαξεν – that is found in the Homeric hymn. The idea of seduction permeates the encounter of Persephone and Hades and is accommodated by the Parisian setting and the French identity of Hades. The repetition of the phrase "I am waiting" by Hades, (ibid., 33) and Persephone's admission that

...he never asked
if I would stay. Which is why,
when the choice appeared
I reached for it.

(ibid., 38)

encapsulate Persephone's process of individuation and maturation as woman. It is not her initiation to sex - this has already happened with "a flat-faced engineering student from Missouri,/a Texan flaunting his teaspoon of Cherokee blood" (ibid., 25) - but her conscious choice to allow herself to be seduced by a man who epitomizes the mystery and allurement of the unknown and the different. Unlike her succumbing to the other men which was the result of curiosity - "I was curious mainly" (ibid., 26) she now decides to assume responsibility for herself by exercising her right of free choice as an adult woman and consent to sex. Dove modernizes the myth of Demeter by deconstructing the traditional relationship between Demeter and Persephone and establishing a democratic and plural context which substitutes the original authoritative one that is found in the previous versions of the myth. Her rendition of the relationship as a process engaging both parties involved constitutes a radical transformation of the original myth and an affirmation of its dynamic quality.

Overall, all three versions present different nuances of a problematic motherhood. By concentrating on loss, the author of the Homeric hymn renders a possessive state of motherhood while Tennyson's emphasis on reunion/εὕρεσις allows for the emergence of an emotionally dependent mother. Finally, Dove's *Mother Love* constitutes a more comprehensive illustration of this problematic motherhood by depicting not only Demeter's possessiveness and dependence as a mother, but also by allowing Persephone's suppressed identity to be heard and her own view and objections to this relationship to be voiced.

A further point of variation in the three versions, which complements and justifies the disparity in the overall mood in the three works, are the feelings of the goddess upon realizing the abduction of her daughter as well as throughout her search for her. While in the Homeric hymn Demeter's most prominent reaction is that of anger, in Tennyson it is her deep sorrow and melancholy that constitute her main reactions to the abduction, and in Dove it is a general feeling of frustration, a mixture of anger, sorrow, confusion and obstinacy, that describes the maternal reaction to the abduction. In the Homeric hymn the very first and immediate feeling that Demeter experiences upon the realization of Persephone's abduction, is agitation and distress, an ἄχος. This ἄχος makes her destroy the veil that was decorating her "ambrosial hair", and throw a blue shawl on her shoulders as an indication of her anguish. However, refusing to compromise with the fact that her daughter has been taken away from her, she does not resort to a passive lamentation: "She sped like an eagle in flight over dry land and water, frenzied, in search of her child." (Sargent 1975, 3)

When Hyperion is trying to explain to her what happened and to appease her, he advises her that "there is no need to nurse this terrible anger" (χολόν) (ibid., 4). Χολός means literally bile, but metaphorically it also connotes the bitterness which is stored in a person's heart and mind. The word therefore suggests an inner psychological as well as a biological anger, a kind of psychosomatic ferocity.

As soon as the goddess realizes that, although her daughter is safe, she will not live with her but with Aidoneus, Demeter experiences the same ἄχος but this time it is a "more piercing and savage" ἄχος (ibid.), "αἰνότερον καὶ κύντερον", which mean more dire and more dog-like.[37] The key word here in appreciating the degree and the intensity of Demeter's anger is the word *κύντερον* which impresses the vivid image of an enraged dog and thus depicts successfully the frantic mood of the goddess. The strong contrast between the *σεμνή* and *ποτνὶα* goddess, and the woman who is overwhelmed by a kind of animalistic anger, is very distinctive. The praise to the awesome goddess becomes at this point the sad report of a woman's frenzied wrath. The question that inevitably arises here is if and how this depiction of the goddess can be explained and justified. The answers to this question are not within the subject matter of this chapter yet an attempt to approach this question is not totally inappropriate either. The anthropomorphic nature of

[37] The word κύντερον is a derivative of the noun *κύων*, gen. *κυνός*, which means dog, adding to the ferocity of the anger.

Greek deities is the immediate and most legitimate response which indeed can account for the wrath and the rather extreme reactions of Demeter. However, the point to be considered is whether these reactions reflect the usual behaviours found in the realm of the mortals or not. Why, for example is there no reference to the fact that the mother is actually missing her beloved daughter, as there is in Tennyson's poem? Why isn't there any insinuation of a maternal sacrifice so that Persephone can return, as in the case of the spousal sacrifice of Alcestis, who volunteers to go to the Underworld instead of her husband. Why isn't there overwhelming pain and sadness, but instead a prevalence of distress, bitterness and anger?

An act demonstrating the goddess's anger is her refraining from the Olympian gatherings as a way of protesting against the authority of Zeus at whom she is furious. In order to make her protest more pronounced she wanders among mortals, indicating in that way her dissatisfaction with, and disregard for, the immortals. Such a reaction can be characterized as childish and hasty but considering the anthropomorphic nature of Greek deities it simply shows the degree of Demeter's anger towards the Olympian conspiracy and, eventually, it highlights her obsessive attachment to her daughter. "Anguish more piercing and savage now entered the heart of Demeter. Enraged by perfidious, black-clouded Zeus son of Cronos, she forsook the assembly of gods and lofty Olympus disguised in form a very long time." (Sargent 1975, 4) The word in the original for enraged is χολωσαμένη (a derivative of χολός) which again indicates the depth and degree of bitterness.

Her final and most extreme reaction to the abduction is her decision to take revenge on Zeus and the rest of the Olympians and not simply rely on her defiance of them. Her decision to destroy the crops, and therefore deprive the Olympians of their sacrificial offerings from the mortals, and thus put the human species in danger of extinction, is indicative of her determination to have her daughter back.

> …. The cruellest of years
> Did the goddess ordain for men on the nourishing earth.
> No seed sprouted in the rich soil, for bright-crowned Demeter lay
> hidden;
> Oxen in vain dragged the bent plows through the fields,
> And white barley was scattered without avail on the ground.
> By terrible famine she would have destroyed the whole race of men
> Endowed with speech, and deprived of their glorious gifts
> Of honour and sacrifice those having homes on Olympus,
> Had not Zeus taken heed and pondered earth's plight in his heart.
>
> (ibid., 9-10)

The "cruellest of years" and the "terrible famine" that she inflicts on humanity depict the degree of her wrath and her bitterness which find an outlet in the affliction caused upon the mortals who have had absolutely no involvement in the abduction.

Even after the intervention of Zeus, who sends Iris to ask the goddess to return to the immortal realm, Demeter is still adamant in her decision.

> So, pleading, she spoke, but Demeter's heart was unmoved.
> Straightway thereafter the father sent forth, one after another,
> All of the blessed gods everlasting, who severally,
> Urged her return. They offered her many gifts
> And of honours among immortals whatever she might care to choose.
> But no one could move her or soften her stubborn heart,
> And she nursed her wrath and, unyielding, rejected their offers.
> Never, she said, would she set foot on fragrant Olympus
> Or send forth the fruits of the earth in their season
> Until she had seen with her own eyes her fair-faced young daughter.
>
> (ibid., 10)

Demeter presents an ultimatum to the Olympians and exhibits such stubborn and rigid behaviour that she is not in the least willing to negotiate with Zeus who despite everything is Persephone's father.

There is an escalation in Demeter's emotions starting from distress progressing to bitterness and finally to a frenzied dog-like anger. Her anguish finds an outlet in the nursing of the infant son of Metaneira and χολός is transformed into the creative activity of the nursing of a child. In fact, this is the only instance in the narrative where Demeter is seen exhibiting such an affectionate and altruistic behaviour to the extent that she attempts to make baby Demophoon immortal.[38] The goddess's willingness to nurse baby Demophoon reveals her desperation to become a nursing mother again. Motherhood apparently has become a way of living for her, and one might even say an addiction: Demeter is addicted to the daily routine of raising a child and seems to be suffering from the deprivation of it. Most significantly, her notion of motherhood seems to be limited to all the practicalities involved and which pertain more to the nursing of a young

[38] It has been argued that this endeavour of hers is an act of retaliation towards Zeus and a defiance of his authority. Demeter has been attributed a feminist and highly political role and has, thus, been interpreted as a subversive female figure and a precursor of the feminist struggle against patriarchy. See Marilyn Arthur 1977, 7-47. Nonetheless, I believe that this is a rather simplistic reading (though quite legitimate to some extent) which does not contribute much to the understanding of Demeter.

child. Had she chosen to look after the daughters of Metaneira (a more relevant task as they are young maidens in need of a female attendant) she would have been engaged with activities such as embroidering, housekeeping, cooking (which again are female activities and are passed on from older women to younger ones). However, such activities hardly presuppose any kind of control on her part, whereas the nursing of an infant is based on the total control of the baby by the mother/nurse.

The story of Demophoon's nursing illustrates the possessive quality that Demetrian motherhood involves. Demeter's reactions of anger, frenzy and stubbornness upon losing Persephone confirm once more the problematic motherhood presented in the Homeric hymn. Her reactions, which are less emotional and more reflexive, are in fact the withdrawal symptoms of her addiction to the routine of mothering.

In Tennyson's poem, Demeter's immediate reactions upon losing her daughter, are neither anger nor emotional derangement but pure sorrow and deep pain. She begins searching for her daughter by asking various animals and elements of nature, whether they wail because of the lost Persephone and this juxtaposition of Demeter with the natural kingdom enhances the motherly desolation (Nath 1992, 129). In fact, there is again a participation of nature in Demeter's distress as there was a participation in her joy in the beginning of the poem.

The jungle rooted in his shatter'd hearth,
The serpent coil'd about his broken shaft,
The scorpion crawling over naked skulls;-
I saw the tiger in the ruin'd fane
Spring from his fallen God, but trace of thee
I saw not;

(Tennyson 1892, 19)

Demeter demonstrates a dignified sorrow and copes with the loss of her beloved daughter in a proud and decent manner. She does not exhibit the wrath and frenzy rendered in the Homeric hymn. It is only towards the end of the poem, when deceived by the gods, through the presentation of a false apparition of Persephone, that she develops bitter feelings towards the Olympians:

Then I, Earth-Goddess, cursed the Gods of heaven.
I would not mingle with their feasts; to me
their nectar smack'd of hemlock on the lips,
their rich ambrosia tasted aconite.

(ibid., 20)

Her refraining from the Olympian congregations is more the result of feelings of disappointment, illustrated in the bitter and poisonous taste of the divine nectar and ambrosia, and not so much the product of anger or annoyance. Tennyson's Demeter loses her trust in the Olympians after they try to deceive her by presenting her with the false apparition of her daughter (so far she was coping with the abduction as an unhappy event which was out of her control but which perhaps she could change in the future). The goddess is obviously upset, but nowhere in the poem do we see her experiencing this χολός and the κύντερον ἄχοςς as well as the desire to retaliate as we see it in the Homeric hymn. Tennyson's Christian framework as well as the Victorian spirit of lamentation can account for this difference in the two texts. Santosh Nath (1992, 40), though, argues that:

> The protagonists of Tennyson's mythical poems on women are a reflection of his ideal of womanhood. The tone of these poems is sombre. Some of them are literary laments, for the poet tries to incorporate in them features of the Greek 'lament'. Others are comparatively free and original in style and form, but a sorrowful mood pervades all of them.

Dignity and endurance as qualities of the ideal woman are not only a Tennysonian resonance but also a Christian and Victorian influence manifested in Demeter as mater dolorosa.[39]

Furthermore, in the Homeric hymn, the sterility of the soil is a result of Demeter's anger towards Zeus and her desire to revenge him. Demeter's plan was to deprive the Olympian gods of the sacrifices they would receive from the products of earth and which was, for them, an affirmation of their authority over the mortals. The arrogance and vanity of the Olympians – manifested in their conspiracy in the abduction of Persephone and in the importance that the sacrificial rituals had for them – can justify to a great extent the wrath of Demeter. However, at that point Demeter is aware that her daughter is safe and, furthermore, – as Hyperion explains to her – she is married to a bridegroom who is neither unsuitable nor disgraceful at all (οὔ τοι ἀεικὴς γαμβρός), is the lord of the immortals (ἐν ἀθανάτοις πολυσημάντωρ) and is ruler of those who live in the Underworld. In addition, Zeus, who is the father of Persephone, has agreed in advance to this marriage and he gives his daughter (ἔδωκε) to Aidoneus. Although Demeter is not aware of this plan and later on does not consent to it, this is

---

[39] Walter Pater (1922, 113-151) also considers Demeter, in the Homeric hymn, the mater dolorosa of the ancient world yet not entirely in the traditional Christian sense but in a rather pagan, mystical sense which relates the Lady of Sorrows to the secret powers of earth and nature.

in accordance with the matrimonial customs of ancient Greece (DeBloois 1997, 246-250). It seems therefore that Demeter's χολός against Zeus is more the bitterness of a mother who realizes that she cannot have control of her daughter anymore.[40] Since Zeus is the one responsible for the execution and success of the abduction plan, her wrath is directed towards him.

In Tennyson though, the sterility of the soil and the destruction of the crops is not a result of the goddess's wish for revenge but it is a participation of nature in her grief.

> My quick tears kill'd the flower, my ravings hush'd
> The bird, and lost in utter grief I fail'd
> To send my life thro' olive-yard and vine
> And golden-grain, my gift to helpless man.
> Rain-rotten died the wheat, the barley-spears
> Were hollow-husk'd, the leaf fell, and the sun,
> Pale at my grief, drew down before his time
> Sickening, and Aetna kept her winter snow.
>
> (Tennyson 1892, 21)

The "quick tears" that "kill'd the flower" in Tennyson contrast greatly with the "The cruelest of years" (Sargent 1975, 9) that the goddess gave to the mortals in the Homeric hymn. In the ancient text we have a deliberate, vindictive destruction of the crops, whereas in the Victorian poem nature shares the deep pain of the mother whose tears destroy the flowers. Furthermore, the earthly sterility is a result of the goddess's unintentional negligence (as opposed to the intentional revenge in the Homeric hymn) of her duties as a protector of agriculture, caused by her great pain.

In short Demeter's reactions in "Demeter and Persephone" are emotionally oriented and revolve around the sorrow and pain that she experiences while deprived of her daughter. Tennyson depicts a highly sentimental and emotionally attached mother who displays great dignity and nobility.

In Rita Dove's poem "The Search", which is the fourth poem of the second book of the collection, and in which the figure of Demeter is introduced, the image of the goddess does not deviate greatly from the

---

[40] In the same essay, Nanci DeBloois (1997, 245-262) argues that Persephone's descent to the Underworld can be seen either as rape or marriage or death since the narrator is impartial and allows both female and male perspectives to be present in the narrative. For Demeter, Persephone's abduction is a rape, and her marriage to Aidoneus equals death (despite the fact that Persephone is an immortal and cannot die in the sense that mortals do).

images in the Homeric hymn and in Tennyson's poem. The first phrase of the poem, "blown apart by loss" (*Mother Love* 1995, 10), highlights the almost annihilating effects of Persephone's abduction on Demeter. The phrase that follows, "she let herself go" (ibid.), indicates the sense of self-abandonment and the desperation of the mother. The succeeding description strongly recalls the two other versions of the myth.

> wandered the neighborhood hatless, breasts
> swinging under a ratty sweater, crusted
> mascara blackening her gaze.
>
> (ibid.)

So far there is no great deviation from the two other versions of the myth with respect to the emotional reactions of Demeter upon the abduction of her daughter. However, Dove's broad perspective of the myth includes the comments of third parties, which eventually function as an expansion of the notion of mother love and of the myth itself. More particularly, in the poem "Grief: The Council", the persona of a friend of Demeter (or for the purposes of Dove's narrative, the Mother) provides an account of the story which contrasts greatly with the image of the Mother rendered in "The Search". In "Grief: The Council", Demeter's mourning and her overall reactions are seen by her friends as an exaggeration and as an indication of her need to be needed.

> I told her: enough is enough.
> Get a hold on yourself, take a lover,
> help some other unfortunate child.
>
> (ibid., 15)

In light of this advice, Demeter's great mourning is seen as an exaggeration and her reactions as a series of melodramatic acts. The loss of Persephone is a tragic situation but not as tragic as Demeter herself sees it. The misfortune of Demeter is not underestimated; however, it is not seen as an ultimate catastrophe either:

> Yes, it's a tragedy, a low-down shame,
> but you still got your own life to live. Meanwhile,
> ain't nothing we can do but be discreet
> and wait
>
> (ibid.)

The poem titled "Mother Love" is a direct and explicit reference to the notion of motherhood as a state of nurturing and being needed. In this poem, we are presented with Demeter's point of view and her decision to nurse Demophoon.

> Who can forget the attitude of mothering?
> Toss me a baby and without bothering
> to blink I'll catch her, sling him on a hip.
> Any woman knows the remedy for grief
> is being needed: duty bugles and we'll
> climb out of exhaustion every time,
> bare the nipple or tuck in the sheet,
> heat milk and hum at bedside until
> they can dress themselves and rise, primed
> for Love or Glory--those one-way mirrors
> girls peer into as their fledging heroes slip
> through, storming the smoky battlefield.
>
> So when this kind woman approached at the urging
> of her bouquet of daughters,
> (one of each of the world's corners,
> one of each of the winds to scatter!)
> and offered up her only male child for nursing
> (a smattering of flesh, noisy and ordinary),
> I put aside the lavish trousseau of the mourner
> for the daintier comfort of pity:
> I decided to save him.

(ibid., 17)

There's no doubt as to the significance of this poem for the mythic transformation of the story of Demeter. There is a straightforward acknowledgement from Demeter herself of her own view of motherhood. For her, motherhood is an "attitude", exhausted in certain routine activities that the nursing of a child involves. Furthermore, she subtly acknowledges the exaggeration of her mourning by referring to that state as "the lavish trousseau of the mourner". Her grief upon losing Persephone has not been a profound experience for her as a mother but it was simply an accessory, or as Scott Ward (1995, 113) articulates it, an "accoutrement". She decides to nurse Demophoon in an attempt to relive the experience of motherhood, since for her, motherhood cannot be understood without the possession and nursing of a child. This "attitude" is more of a mechanical performance of daily tasks rather than a relationship. Rita Dove indeed deconstructs the "myth" of Demeter and reveals a more realistic and more human aspect of it.

Again here, as in the Homeric hymn, we are not given the profound emotional implications of the abduction of Persephone for her mother. Demeter is not considering her daughter's point of view, namely her desire to "grow up" (*Mother Love* 1995, 7) and learn to live far from her mother's protection. Instead she "wandered the neighbourhood hatless," (ibid., 10) an image which suggests a state of mental agitation; again there is no reference to pain and genuine maternal concern.

In *Mother Love* Demeter is presented as a highly frustrated mother who reacts with anger, grief, frenzy, depression and exaggeration when her daughter is not with her any more. Dove achieves a twentieth-century metamorphosis of the original myth and unveils a so far hidden aspect of it: the fallacious quality of Demetrian motherhood and the demystification of the goddess as the symbol of motherhood.

The Homeric hymn ends with the prospect that every year Persephone will ascend to visit her mother and renew the hope for the continuation of life. The ending is rather abrupt and perhaps even anticlimactic, since from the gloomy atmosphere of Demeter's wrath we are suddenly transferred to the joyous atmosphere of the Eleusinian mysteries. It is noteworthy that although the goddess is still distressed, even at the moment of reunion – dreading the possibility of Persephone having eaten the pomegranate seed and therefore having to spend one third of the year with Hades – and despite the confirmation of her initial fear, she celebrates the return of Persephone and invites humanity to rejoice with her. The hymn ends with the initiation of humanity to the knowledge and secrets of life.

Tennyson introduces the idea of Christian love which humanizes the myth, and he advocates the optimism that death is followed by resurrection in a world of Love.

> Henceforth, as having risen from out the dead,
> Shalt ever send thy life along with mine
> From buried grain thro' springing blade, and bless
> Their garner'd autumn also, reap with me,
> Earth-Mother, in the harvest hymns of Earth
> the worship which is Love, …

(Tennyson 1892, 23)

Tennyson advocates a belief in Christian love as a painful but also hopeful experience. The knowledge and practice of "the worship which is Love" not only elevates humanity but it further provides an existential and, one might say, theosophical alternative to his contemporary social and intellectual predicament in a manner that the poet illustrates in "In Memoriam".

In the two versions of the myth (the Homeric hymn and Tennyson's poem) we have quite different aspects of Demetrian motherhood. What the two texts have in common is the strong desire for and attachment to the child. The Homeric hymn, however, illustrates the stubborn adherence to the child while Tennyson's poem exhibits a more genuine love and concern for the well-being of the child, despite the great degree of emotional dependence on the part of the mother.

Rita Dove concludes with a harmonious resolution of the separation of Persephone from her mother. After gaining knowledge of the world and of herself away from her mother, Persephone becomes a mother herself (this is recounted in the poem "History") and the relationship of the two women enters a new stage. Persephone has managed to stand on her own feet and Demeter has begun to learn to lead a meaningful life without her daughter. In "Demeter's Prayer to Hades" she advises Hades to try to achieve personal harmony and integration: "Believe in yourself, go ahead – see where it gets you." (Dove 1995, 63) Self-knowledge and individuation are not only Persephone's eventual achievements but also Demeter's, who undergoes a coming-of-age experience and transforms her frustration into knowledge of herself, of life and of genuine maternal love.

Demetrian motherhood, as distilled from the comparative study of the three versions of the classical myth, is a troublesome and problematic concept which often operates as a disguise for dependence, possession, control and the need for self-assertion and self-fulfilment.

In the following pages, I wish to explore Demetrian motherhood as it is manifested in Federico García Lorca's play *Yerma* and try to identify its significance and contribution to the interpretation of the play and, more particularly, to the character of Yerma. In other words, I shall attempt to show how motherhood for Yerma is a disguise for her problematic marriage and a vain attempt to achieve self-fulfilment and self-assertion. Motherhood for Yerma is a highly idealized state and is seen as a panacea for her desolate marital state. Just like Demeter, the quintessential mother, Yerma finds in the idea of motherhood, or rather mothering, a substitute for her personal needs of fulfilment and self-identity. Demetrian motherhood as a means, and not an end in itself, is also a quality of Yerma whose obstinacy over children is not as wholehearted as readers and critics tend to assume. Both women have a similar attitude to motherhood and they both adhere to it and use it as a camouflage for their unfulfilled and incomplete personalities. First, I will show Yerma's dissatisfaction with Juan on a physical and sexual level and then I will discuss how motherhood is an alibi for Yerma's discontent with Juan and with herself in this marriage.

When Federico García Lorca first read the play at the home of Carlos Morla Lynch on the 3rd of December 1934, Morla himself described it as "terrible and beautiful" (Edwards 1980, 167). The beauty of the play, is apart from the poetry, the representation of the latent yet ardent desire of the heroine for a passionate intercourse. The element of terror in the tragedy is the idea that if this desire is not fulfilled it can turn into a destructive power.

Let us examine then the fallacy of Yerma's apprehension of motherhood. First and foremost, Yerma is totally unhappy with Juan as her sexual and marital companion. She is neither physically attracted to him nor in any way associated with him on an emotional, mental or spiritual level. The opening scene of the play is an idyllic one, where Yerma is asleep while a shepherd enters the stage holding a child dressed in white. As soon as they exit, Yerma wakes up and sings a nursery song. This passing of the shepherd with the child can undoubtedly be interpreted as Yerma's dream while asleep and consequently the scene functions as an insight into her unconscious directly conveying the idea that she yearns for a child. Interestingly enough, the child in her dream is not alone (a fact which would signify the importance of motherhood) neither is it accompanied by Juan whose presence in Yerma's dream would be more than legitimate since he is her husband. The child is accompanied by a shepherd, insinuating thus Yerma's unconscious desire not simply for a child but for a child from Victor, the shepherd to whom she is sexually attracted, as it is subsequently revealed in the play. The image of the shepherd holding a child by the hand signifies the fusion of motherhood and sexuality and proclaims the tragic struggle of the heroine between the two states. This struggle is in fact her true struggle vacillating between her improper desire for Victor and the desire she is expected to have for Juan (Mabrey 1996, 36). Motherhood becomes simply a disguise for Yerma's sexual frustration since she chooses to remain with Juan.

In the following scene Yerma's husband, Juan, enters, and she immediately expresses her secret wish that he were as vivacious, effervescent and vigorous as every young man of his age.

> YERMA. ¿No tomas un vaso de leche?
> JUAN. ¿Para qué?
> YERMA. Trabajas mucho y no tienes tú cuerpo para resistir los trabajos.
> JUAN. Cuando los hombres se quedan enjutos se ponen fuertes como el acero.
> YERMA. Pero tú no. Cuando nos casamos eras otro. Ahora tienes la cara blanca como si no te diera en ella el sol. A mí me gustaría que fueras al

> río y nadaras y que te subieras al tejado cuando la lluvia cala nuestra vivienda. Veinticuatro meses llevamos casados y tú cada vez más triste, más enjuto, como si crecieras al revés. (Lorca 1956, 12)

> YERMA. Won't you have a glass of milk?
> JUAN. What for?
> YERMA. You work a lot and your body's not strong enough for it.
> JUAN. When men grow thin they get strong as steel.
> YERMA. But not you. You were different when we were first married. Now you've got a face as white as though the sun had never shone on it. I'd like to see you go to the river and swim or climb up on the roof when the rain beats down on our house. Twenty-four months we've been married and you only get sadder, thinner, as if you were growing backwards. (Lorca 1976, 279-280)

This scene indicates that apart from Yerma's wish for a child there is also a serious breakdown in their relationship. Yerma obviously wants a vigorous and virile husband who is an integral part of nature and, as such, possesses the juices and the vivacity of nature. As Rupert Allen points out in his book, *Psyche and Symbol in the Theater of Federico García Lorca*, (1974, 132) "Yerma voices her anxieties and suggests that perhaps he is lacking the requisite vigor." Moreover, she is patronizing her husband by projecting her own fantasies about her ideal man onto him: "I'd like to see you…" In the original text the word that Yerma uses for different is otro, which means other, another.[41] The word otro suggests Yerma's unconscious wish that her husband were another man, un otro hombre. Yerma does not accept Juan for what he is but retains a desire for what she would have liked him to be. Her words betray her lack of admiration for, acceptance of, and eventually, attraction towards Juan. Her view of Juan is that of an outcast of the male species to whom the perennial laws of nature, applicable to all other men, do not apply; thus he is "growing backwards". Juan's marginalization and exclusion, not by the local male community but by his own wife, highlights Yerma's utter rejection and resentment of her husband. Not only is she not happy with his physical appearance and overall vigour, but she considers him a mistake of nature, an unnatural and flawed member of the male species. Through her comments she rejects him as her partner and wishes she had another (otro) man as her husband. Her rejection of him as her sexual partner is confirmed later on when she speaks with the Old

---

[41] "Cuando nos casamos eras otro", *Lorca, Obras Completas*, ed. Guillermo De Torre 1956, 12. Otro as an adjective means other, another and as a pronoun means another one.

Woman, the Vieja, and confesses her lack of sexual attraction to him while suggesting that this other man, this otro hombre is Victor the shepherd.[42]

When Juan gets upset by these comments, Yerma very cleverly attempts to disguise her dislike for her husband by presenting her concern for his vigour as a concern for his health.

> YERMA. No lo tomes a mal. Si yo estuviera enferma me gustaría que tú me cuidases. "Mi mujer está enferma. Voy a matar este cordero para hacerle un buen quiso de carne. Mi mujer está enferma. Voy a guardar esta enjundia de gallina para aliviar su pecho, voy a llevarle esta piel de oveja para guardar sus pies de la nieve." Así soy yo. Por eso te cuido. (Lorca 1956, 13)

> YERMA. Don't take it wrong. If I were sick I'd like you to take care of me. "My wife's sick. I'm going to butcher this lamb and cook her a good meat dish". "My wife's sick. I'm going to save this chicken-fat to relieve her chest; I'm going to take her this sheepskin to protect her feet from the snow". That's the way I am. That's why I take care of you. (Lorca 1976, 280)

Yerma is conscious of her own inability to feel any kind of attraction towards Juan and therefore consistently tries to conceal it. She feels guilty when her behaviour gives away her true feelings for him and she attempts to compensate with an expression of a seemingly spousal concern for him.

Juan, on the other hand, rejects her argument by stating that he is simply overworking and getting older, something which happens to everybody: "Because there's nothing wrong with me. All these things are just your imagination. I work hard. Each year I'll get older." (ibid.)

Continuing her efforts to wipe out any suspicion that her comments might have raised in Juan's mind, Yerma later on declares that she loves him providing as proof of her love her anticipation of her wedding night and her total lack of fear, which was unlike all other girls: "No one ever got married with more happiness." (ibid.).

Juan refuses to listen, offended by her commentary on his virility and vivacity. In fact, he tells her to shut up (Calla*)*, a word which, indicates the degree to which he feels offended and emotionally wounded. It can be argued that Juan's refusal to listen to his wife's speech about her love for him, is due to his strict, patriarchal nature which makes him unresponsive

---

[42] The text is clear as to Yerma's attraction to Victor, the shepherd. While speaking to the Old Woman she admits that once, when Victor held her in his arms to carry her across a stream, she trembled. Gustavo Correa (1962, 97) suggests that Victor's decision to sell his livestock and go away is an indication that "perhaps he himself suffers a conflict which he prefers to resolve by fleeing from the danger."

towards women's emotions considering them worthless and insignificant.[43] However, Juan is not the typical patriarchal man; he is happy without offsprings and does not wish to be the patriarch of a traditional big family. Moreoever, his only requirement regarding his wife is that she stays at home and performs her duties as a housewife while he performs his duties as a working husband. For Juan this kind of division of labor does not aim at restricting Yerma or asserting his authority over her; on the contrary it reflects his belief of how a household should be managed.

Yerma's subsequent attempt to embrace and kiss him is not her expression of love, but an attempt to cleanse her own guilt for not feeling attracted to him, a guilt which she probably became conscious of as soon as she uttered her comments on his strength and vivacity which gave away her dislike for him and offended him as well. In 1930s' Andalusian Spain, where the concept of machismo is almost synonymous with maleness, even a slight insinuation of a man's possible deviation from the established image of manliness constitutes an enormous and serious offence. Yerma is aware of that, and her reference to Juan's insubstantial virility is a clear indicator of the degree of her feeling of repulsion for him and her sexual dissatisfaction in her marriage. Her comments reveal a woman with a strong sense of sexuality; her description of Juan (or rather the otro hombre she is fantasizing about) swimming in the river or climbing on the roof of their house, shows her appreciation of physical strength and vivacity in man. But they also portray a woman deprived of sexual satisfaction and fulfilment. Juan does not possess either the physical or the sexual virility that Yerma wants her partner to have.

Yerma subsequently attempts to dismiss her guilt by attributing the idea of Juan's physical inadequacy to the other villagers while declaring that she does not share their views. However, her short speech betrays pity for Juan and once again illustrates her negative view of him.

> JUAN. Calla. Demasiado trabajo tengo yo con oír en todo momento…
> YERMA. No. No me repitas lo que dicen. Yo veo por mis ojos que eso no puede ser…A fuerza de caer la lluvia sobre las piedras éstas ablandan y hacen crecer jaramagos, que las gentes dicen que no sirven para nada. Los jaramagos no sirven para nada, pero yo bien los veo mover sus flores amarillas en el aire. (Lorca 1956, 15)

---

[43] Juan can be seen as a representative of the traditional patriarchal status quo of rural Spain and perceived as an oppressor of Yerma's personality and sexuality. Subsequently, Yerma's struggle can be seen as the struggle against male patriarchal dominion.

> JUAN. Hush! I have a hard enough job hearing all the time that I'm...
> YERMA. No. Don't tell me what they say. I can see with my own eyes that that isn't so. The rain just by the force of its falling on the stones softens them and makes weeds grow – weeds which people say aren't good for anything. "Weeds aren't good for anything," yet I see them plainly enough – moving their yellow flowers in the wind. (Lorca 1976, 280-281)

The metaphor of the weeds betrays Yerma's view of Juan as somebody insignificant, inferior and worthy of her pity, and she is once again patronizing him. Her words betray a great contempt for him while they affirm her own sense of superiority: Juan is simply not good enough for her, he is not manly enough for her in the bedroom and in life.

The beginning of the play lays the parameters within which the tragedy evolves. Juan does not seem to fulfil Yerma's expectations of a husband and, most importantly, she does not come to terms with it. Moreover, she does not rest on the idea that she can neither change her husband nor her feelings for him. This refusal of hers to compromise constitutes the point of departure for the tragedy. Her persistent refusal to compromise with her marital predicament is highlighted by the character of the young married girl who, although in the same situation as Yerma, has totally given up hope and has adopted a humorous attitude towards her life and her marriage. "Look, I'm going to take my husband his food", she laughs. "That's something to see! Too bad I can't say my sweetheart, isn't it?" She laughs ... (ibid., 292) The young girl has submitted to her own marital predicament and cannot even hypocritically call her husband her sweetheart.[44] Unlike her, Yerma is profoundly disturbed by the fact that she does not like Juan as a man or lover and she wishes she could have been able to do so. Her suffering is rooted in the fact that she does not and cannot feel sexual attraction for and satisfaction with Juan and she is unwilling to give up the idea of achieving a sexually fulfilling marriage: she wants what she cannot have.

Following her intense discussion with Juan, Yerma meets her friend Maria, who announces her pregnancy. The conversation revolves around motherhood and it appears that although motherhood seems to be Yerma's only concern, sexual desire and pleasure are latent concerns asserting thus the fusion of sexuality and motherhood that was rendered in the opening scene of the play. Yerma wants to know how Maria knew that she was

---

[44] The word for sweetheart in the original is novio, which literally means lover, boyfriend, and implies an emotional and physical correspondence.

pregnant and the answer she receives is a reminder of her own miserable situation:

> MARIA. No sé. Pero la noche que nos casamos me lo decía constantemente con su boca puesta en mi mejilla, tanto que a mí me parece que mi niño es un palomo de lumbre que él me deslizó por la oreja. (Lorca 1956, 20)
>
> MARIA. I don't know. But on our wedding night he kept telling me about it with his mouth pressed against my cheek; so that now it seems to me my child is a dove of fire he made slip in through my ear. (Lorca 1976, 284)

Maria's husband has obvious passion for his wife and the image of him pressing his mouth against her cheek and whispering his desire to her communicates the passionate atmosphere between them during their sexual intercourse. This image contrasts greatly with the image that Yerma projects about her intercourse with Juan, where she lies in bed "looking at the ceiling with sad eyes" while Juan quickly finishes his duty and then "turns over and goes to sleep" (ibid., 290). For J. Alberich (1965, 32) this phrase encapsulates Yerma's unhappiness and dissatisfaction in her marriage and is a precise and acute rendition of her psychological state as a wife and a woman. Christopher Brian Weimer (1992, 523) draws a very interesting parallel between Lorca's Yerma and Tennessee Williams's Maggie, pointing out that one of their basic differences is the fact that Yerma has not achieved sexual fulfilment while Maggie is in tune with her sexuality. "Yerma is a woman stifling her own sexuality, while Maggie's is stifled by Brick's refusal to sleep with her." Maggie can experience sexual desire with Brick, and her problem is that he refuses to sleep with her any longer. On the other hand, Yerma cannot experience desire although she has regular sexual intercourse with Juan. Thus she says to Maria: "Oh, how lucky you are!" (Lorca 1976, 284) Ironically, Maria assumes that Yerma's sexual knowledge is greater than hers: "But you know more about these things." (ibid.) The two women refer to two completely different experiences. As Parilla (1995, 116) points out: "Maria speaks about lovemaking; Yerma attends to the mechanics of procreation." (Arturi Parilla 1995, 116) Sexuality and motherhood are once again presented in inextricable relation to each other. Maria's pregnancy comes as a natural result of her passionate reciprocal love-making with her husband, thus creating a link between motherhood and sexuality.

The scene with the old woman, the Vieja provides a significant insight into Yerma's marital desolation and constitutes a moment of revelation in the play. The character of the Vieja, who is a sexually fulfilled woman and represents healthy and natural sexuality, accentuates Yerma's desperation.

The Vieja has known and has enjoyed carnal delights and talks very positively about marriage: "Men have got to give us pleasure, girl. They've got to take down our hair and let us drink water out of their mouths." (ibid., 289) "Who can say that this body we've got isn't beautiful?" (ibid., 288) Her philosophy is simple: you must love and desire your man, and children come naturally as a result of this; it is not mechanical intercourse that produces children but desire and pleasure (Degoy 1999, 165). Yerma's lack of passion in her copulation with Juan is evident in her dialogue with the Vieja:

VIEJA. Oye. ¿A ti te gusta tu marido?
YERMA. ¿Cómo?
VIEJA. Que si lo quieres Si deseas estar con él…
YERMA. No sé.
VIEJA. ¿No tiemblas cuando se acerca a ti? ¿No te da así como un sueño cuando acerca sus labios? Dime.
YERMA. No. No lo he sentido nunca. (Lorca 1956, 29)

VIEJA. Listen: Does your husband please you?
YERMA. What?
VIEJA. I mean-do you really love him? Do you long to be with him?
YERMA. I don't know.
VIEJA. Don't you tremble when he comes near you? Don't you feel something like a dream when he brings his lips close to yours? Tell me.
YERMA. No. I've never noticed it. (Lorca 1976, 289)

Yerma's oblivion to sexual arousal and orgasmic intercourse reveals her total lack of such experiences. The equation of love and sexual desire that the Vieja articulates accentuates Yerma's marital void: she is a woman empty of love and sexuality. However, she is able to experience some sexual excitement albeit not with Juan.

YERMA. *Recordando.* Quizá…Una vez… Víctor…
VIEJA. Sigue.
YERMA. Me cogió de la cintura y no pude decirle nada porque no podía hablar. Otra vez el mismo Víctor, teniendo yo catorce años (él era un zagalón), me cogió en sus brazos para saltar una acequia y me entró un temblor que me sonaron los dientes. Pero es que yo he sido vergonzosa. (Lorca 1956, 29-30)

YERMA, *Remembering.* Perhaps …. one time … with Victor….
VIEJA. Go on.
YERMA. He took me by the waist and I couldn't say a word to him, because I couldn't talk. Another time this same Victor, when I was fourteen years

> old – he was a husky boy – took me in his arms to leap a ditch and I started shaking so hard my teeth chattered. But I've always been shy. (Lorca 1976, 289)

A simple touch by Victor manages to elicit sensations that years of intercourse with Juan have not managed to achieve. There is no frustration with Victor but on the contrary there is the certainty of sensual excitement. With Victor, Yerma "felt that which Juan never managed to achieve: the natural, instinctive attraction which precedes maternity." (Machado Bonet de Benvenuto 1951, 117) This juxtaposition accentuates Yerma's predicament as a mismatched and unhappy woman who is not attracted to her husband and is not in the least sexually satisfied by him.

Further into the play Yerma and Juan are engaged in a very intense conversation, during which Yerma expresses her complaints openly and vehemently and Juan provides his point of view of their marriage. The scene opens with Juan interrogating his two sisters about his wife's absence from the house. As soon as she returns home and tells her "Don't you know my way of thinking? The sheep in the fold and women at home" (Lorca 1976, 305), she seizes the opportunity to articulate her own dissatisfaction with their relationship.

> YERMA. Justo. Las mujeres dentro de sus casas. Cuando las casas no son tumbas. Cuando las sillas se rompen y las sábanas de hilo se gastan con el uso. Pero aquí no. Cada noche, cuando me acuesto, encuentro mi cama más nueva, más reluciente, como si estuviera recién traída de la cuidad. (Lorca 1956, 57)

> YERMA. Justly. Women in their homes. When those homes aren't tombs. When the chairs break and the linen sheets wear out with use. But not here. Each night, when I go to bed, I find my bed newer, more shining – as if it had just been brought from the city. (Lorca 1976, 305)

Yerma has no objection to the patriarchal status quo and the division of labor that Juan suggests – men at work, women at home. Her problem is that her own house is a tomb, as she says, and a constant reminder of her own miserable situation. The chairs that have not broken are an insinuation of the absence of children. However, in this short speech of hers, the emphasis is not on children but on the bed which signifies the importance of her sexual life for her marriage and for her own well-being. The bed, the linen sheets of which, have not been worn out with use, becomes the centre of her marriage and eventually the centre of her life. The fact that the bed, as a physical object, becomes newer, reversing thus the natural process of physical decay and dilapidation, is an indicator of the unnaturalness of the relationship between Juan and Yerma. Their bed, as a symbol of union between the two spouses, becomes for Yerma the very grave of her sexuality and her womanhood. Yerma resorts to itinerancy and wanders in the streets not because she is seeking adultery as Juan believes, but because her house has become the tomb of her very identity, and she embarks on a quest for her lost self. This image resonates with Rita Dove's Demeter who "wandered the neighbourhoods hatless" (Dove 1995, 10) ostensibly in search of her child but in fact in quest of her own identity. The metaphor of vagrancy signifies for both women their search for individuation and self-awareness.[45]

At this point in the play, Yerma's lack of sexual attraction towards Juan, as well as her lack of sexual fulfilment, are well-established. The name Yerma which means barren but also empty and dry and deserted, now implies the heroine's sexual emptiness and the sexual drought to which her body is condemned.

Yerma's sexual drought is expressed not only in her name but in her own words when she declares:

> Quiero beber agua y no hay vaso ni agua, quiero subir al monte y no tengo pies, quiero bordar mis enaguas y no encuentro los hilos. (Lorca 1956, 59)
>
> I want to drink water and there's neither water nor a glass. I want to go up the mountain, and I have no feet. I want to embroider skirts and I can't find thread. (Lorca 1976, 307)

The water imagery – frequently employed throughout the play – signifies the desiccation of her sexuality, whereas the walk to the mountain signifies the lack of vivacity. The embroidered skirts signify the lack of imagination and recreation in her life. Yerma's diction betrays the sexual and emotional drought that she experiences.

The centrality of Yerma's sexuality is very apparent when she utters a cry of existential anguish concerning her identity as a woman. "I don't know what I am. Let me walk around; get myself in hand again." (ibid.)

Her dissatisfaction with Juan reaches the point of the annulment of their marriage in the sense that since there is no desire in it and no offspring to compensate for the absence of sexuality, Juan and Yerma are simply sharing the same roof. When Juan tells her to remember that she is a married woman and should not engage in conversations with men on the street, Yerma

---

[45] This motif of vagrancy, as a metaphor for the search for self-awareness, is also present in *The Great Chimera* (discussed in Chapter Three) where Marina wanders in the streets of Syros late at night seemingly in search of a lover but actually in search of her own identity as a woman.

exclaims with great surprise: "Married!" (ibid.) In response Juan shifts the discussion towards a moral direction by bringing up the issue of family honour.

A very telling scene takes place in the second Act, Scene one, where the group of Andalusian women, which functions as a chorus, comment on Yerma as a promiscuous and unfaithful wife.[46]

> LAVANDERA 4ª. Yo planté un tomillo, yo lo vi crecer.
> El que quiera honra que se porte bien.
>
> (Lorca 1956, 44)

> Fourth Levandera. I planted thyme,
> I watched it grow.
> Who wants a good name
> Must live just so.
>
> (Lorca 1976, 297)

Later on, the same laundress (Levandera) clearly articulates Yerma's "infidelity":

> A uno, ¿lo oyes? Entérate tú, ¿quieres que lo diga mas alto? (Risas) Y cuando no lo mira, porque está sola, porque no lo tiene delante, lo lleva retratado en los ojos. (Lorca 1956, 47)

> Someone. Haven't you heard? You find out for yourself. Do you want me to say it louder? (laughter) And when she's not looking at him – when she's alone, when he's not right in front of her – she carries his picture-in her eyes. (Lorca 1976, 299)

Yerma's "good name" has been spoiled because she looks at Victor in a lustful way that betrays her feeling for him. For Andalusian morality (represented here by the Levanderas, especially the fourth one), infidelity does not only consist of consummation but also of the mere desire, the unconsummated but fervent passion that manifests itself in the way one

---

[46] Lorca himself has labelled the play a tragedy and, indeed, the theme as well as the structure and characterisation have strong resonances of Classical tragedy:
Yerma will be the tragedy of the sterile woman. The theme as you know is classical. But I want to give it a new development and intent. A tragedy with four principal characters and a chorus, as all tragedies should have.
See Lima 1963, 217-218 and Lacalle Martinez 1988, 227-237. Furthermore, the subtitle of the play is "Poema tragico en tres actos y seis cuadros".

looks at the object of desire. When Yerma looks at Victor she does so in a way that expresses all her suppressed sexuality and her wish for sexual fulfilment. As the fourth laundress says:

> Hay una cosa en el mundo que es la mirada. Mi madre lo decía. No es lo mismo una mujer mirando unas rosas que una mujer mirando los muslos de un hombre. Ella lo mira. (Lorca 1956, 46)

> In this world just a glance can be something. My mother always said that. A woman looking at roses isn't the same thing as a woman looking at a man's thighs. And she looks at him. (Lorca 1976, 299)

Not only is Yerma looking at Victor in a sexual way but she also "carries his picture – in her eyes" in the sense that her sexual attraction towards him is not a carnal, superficial one that is elicited upon a glance at this image and vanishes as soon as he leaves: on the contrary it is a profound and constant desire that she feels for him. Thus "she carries his picture – in her eyes" and fantasizes about him; her comments on how she would like Juan to swim in the river and climb on the roof can be seen as a possible projection of one of her fantasies about Victor.

The scene with the Levanderas signifies Yerma's isolation from her community. As Lima (1963, 230) notes, "Wrought in the tradition of Greek tragedy, this scene serves to accentuate Yerma's unsought separation from her neighbours, from tradition, hence from society itself." Yerma is indeed an outcast since she neither compromises nor is she willing to do something about her desolate marital state. The characters of the Vieja and the Muchacha emphasize her isolation and her differentiation from the female community.

In the scene of Victor's farewell, Yerma does not hesitate to show her feelings for him and therefore validate her own dissatisfaction with Juan as a partner.

> YERMA. Víctor.
> VICTOR. Dime.
> YERMA. ¿Por qué te vas? Aquí las gentes te quieren.
> VICTOR. Yo me porté bien. *(Pausa.)*
> YERMA. Te portaste bien. Siendo zagalón me llevaste una vez en brazos, ¿no recuerdas? Nunca se sabe lo que va a pasar.
> VICTOR. Todo cambia
> YERMA. Algunas cosas no cambian. Hay cosas encerradas detrás de los muros que no pueden cambiar porque nadie las oye.
> VICTOR: Así es. (Lorca 1956, 68-69)

YERMA. Victor.
VICTOR. Yes?
YERMA. Why are you going away? The people here like you.
VICTOR. I've behaved myself.
Pause.
YERMA. You always behave yourself. When you were a boy, you carried me once in your arms, do you remember that? One never knows what's going to happen.
VICTOR. Everything changes
YERMA. Some things never change. There are things shut up behind walls that can't change because nobody hears them
VICTOR. That's how things are. (Lorca 1976, 312)

The "things shut up behind walls" are nothing but Yerma's desire for her own sexuality which she can experience with Victor. Victor seems to be hesitant to reciprocate Yerma's feelings for him: "The tension between them is even worse because they are attracted to each other, they are conscious of the electricity, the heat, the sweet memories. Victor refuses to listen to them and he listens only to Yerma." (Degoy 1999, 171)[47] The departure of Victor also signifies the departure of symbolic eros, love and fertility (Anderson 1984, 114). Yerma's last hope, the otro hombre she dreams of, vanishes leaving her fantasies devoid of their object.

In the subsequent discussion with Maria, Yerma again raises the issue of her "dry" existence by using water imagery.

YERMA. Las mujeres cuando tenéis hijos no podéis pensar en las que no los tenemos. Os quedáis frescas, ignorantes como el que nada en agua dulce no tiene idea de la sed. (Lorca 1956, 63)

YERMA. You women who have children can't think about us who don't! You stay always fresh, with no idea of it, just as anyone swimming in fresh water has no idea of thirst. (Lorca 1976, 309)

And almost immediately she adds: "Each time I have more desire and less hope." (ibid.)

Yerma gradually loses her sense of her own sexuality and femininity because there is nothing in her relationship with Juan to elicit and cultivate her sexuality. She feels totally deprived of her womanhood and she cries: "I

[47] Susana Degoy (1999, 131-140 and 162-223) looks at *Blood Wedding, Yerma* and *The House of Bernada Alba* as the "Trilogy of confinement" and discusses Yerma's entrapment in her loveless and desiccated marriage. For Degoy, Yerma's predicament is enveloped in her own admission that she is at "the darkest pit of the well" – "ahora que estoy entrado en lo más oscuro del pozo".

wish I were a woman" (ibid., 295). She experiences the loss of her female identity, not only on an emotional and mental level but also on a physical one: she begins to think of herself as a man.

> YERMA. Muchas noches bajo yo a echar la comida a los bueyes, que antes no lo hacía, porque ninguna mujer lo hace y cuando paso por lo oscuro del cobertizo mis pasos me suenan a pasos de hombre. (Lorca 1956, 64)

> YERMA. Many nights I go down to feed the oxen – which I never did before, because no woman does it – and when I pass through the darkness of the shed my footsteps sound to me like the footsteps of a man. (Lorca 1976, 309)

Yerma's self-alienation reaches the point of an absolute emotional frustration in which she identifies herself with the son she desires to have. "I'll end up believing I'm my own son." (ibid.) This identification with a potential child of hers is an indicator of her own incomplete identity and resonates with Demeter's identification with Persephone. Demeter's search for Persephone can be seen as a metaphor for her own search for individual identity and in the light of her quest, Yerma's quest for a child echoes her search for an identity. Demeter realizes her true quest when addressing Hades:

> This alone is what I wish for you: knowledge. To understand that each desire has an edge, to know we are responsible for the lives we change. (Dove 1995, 63)

Demeter's final realization of the need for individuation and self-awareness determines Yerma's quest as well. Yerma desires the knowledge of a passionate relationship with Juan, which is also for her the knowledge of herself. Her questions to the Vieja, "... I want to find out. Yes you can tell me." (Lorca 1976, 288), her visit to the sorceress's house, and finally to the pagan feast, the Romeria, manifest her desire for knowledge. This knowledge pertains to sexuality but it also encompasses the sphere of human relationships and of self-consciousness. Yerma lacks the knowledge of lust, love and eventually of her own self. Her inability to experience a passionate relationship with Juan is symbolized in her inability to "sing" while with Juan, and signifies her ultimate loss of identity (Greenfield 1981, 19).[48] Obsession with motherhood becomes for both women the substitute

[48] The importance of female singing as a metaphor for an enjoyable and gratifying sexual intercourse is mentioned by Greenfield (1981, 18-21) as an indication of Yerma's lack of sexual pleasure, as opposed to Maria's satisfaction in her sex life.

for their lost identity and the alibi for their oblivion to what constitutes the real loss in their lives. Lamentation and grief for the loss of a child is actually the mourning for lost identity. Dove's Demeter openly acknowledges this fallacy by admitting, "Any woman knows the remedy for grief is being needed" (*Mother Love* 1995, 17) although it is only in the end that she becomes capable of incorporating this realization into her motherly behaviour. Yerma, however, fails to achieve this self-knowledge and remains within the constraints of her frustration and bitterness until the very end. Although she thinks that her problem is the absence of a child in her life, she fails to acknowledge the fact that she lacks sexual fulfilment and this makes her feel like a man. Had she been able to bear a child, would she have managed to feel "a woman" as she wishes?

The discussion with Maria further reveals Yerma's notion of motherhood. She seems to have idealized and individualized idea of motherhood. When, for example, Maria mentions that as her pregnancy advances, the baby will start kicking, Yerma immediately makes a rather exaggerated statement: "And that's, when you love him best, when you can really say: 'My child!'" (ibid., 283) At this point Yerma speaks with the certainty of a woman who has already been pregnant and knows the feelings that the kicking of the baby can elicit for the mother. However, motherhood for her is a private notion that she has constructed and has been cultivating in her mind, and thus Gustavo Correa (1957, 87) justly calls her "una madre virtual", a virtual mother. Yerma's melodramatic statements echo Tennyson's Demeter who tries to identify with mothers from the world of nature because she is also "una madre virtual". After Persephone's abduction Demeter becomes a virtual mother and her feelings of adherence to and dependence on her daughter intensify. The attempt to nurse Demophoon is in fact a desperate attempt to escape this state of virtual motherhood and enter the state of actual motherhood which, according to Demeter, consists of the practicalities involved in child nursing. However, this virtual motherhood still continues for Demeter since she realizes that her powers over Demophoon are limited as she is only his nurse and it is actually his mother who has the last word about him.[49] Yerma clings to this virtual motherhood and her whole life and existence revolves around it. She imagines, or rather fantasizes about, the feeling of being pregnant, about the bites of the baby while breastfeeding, and even hallucinates about children.

---

[49] Nancy Felson-Rubin and Harriet M. Deal (1994, 190-197) argue that the whole Demophoon episode facilitates the concentration on the character of Demeter and signifies the changes in her, i.e. her realization that although a goddess she has some limitations.

As she has lost every hope of sexual fulfilment she has turned to motherhood as an alternative. Parilla (1995, 116) claims that motherhood has become a matter of life and death for her: "Motherhood is the only thing that can define her: denial of it becomes a denial of self." (Arturi Parilla 1995, 116)

Yerma later on explains that motherhood involves the sacrifice of having to nurse a child:

> MARIA. Dicen que con los hijos se sufre mucho.
> YERMA. Mentira. Eso lo dicen las madres débiles, las quejumbrosas. ¿Para que los tienen? Tener un hijo no es tener un ramo de rosas. Hemos de sufrir para verlos crecer. (Lorca 1956, 22)

> MARIA. They say one suffers a lot with children.
> YERMA. That's a lie. That's what weak, complaining mothers say. What do they have them for? Having a child is no bouquet of roses. We must suffer to see them grow. (Lorca 1976, 285)

Yerma here presents a melodramatic and exaggerated version of motherhood. She perceives the experience of motherhood as a state of suffering and tolerating the trivialities involved in upbringing, and in fact she considers this maternal suffering a prerequisite for the raising of children. This view strongly resembles the view that Dove's Demeter/Mother has concerning motherhood when she mentions that "duty bugles and we'll climb out of exhaustion every time" (*Mother Love* 1995, 17). As a matter of fact, Yerma articulates the same idea when she states that "Having a child is no bouquet of roses". Interestingly enough, neither of them refers to the emotional experience of having children and its implications on a woman. Apparently, both Yerma and Demeter/Mother choose to focus on the act of nursing and see it as a form of martyrdom. Demeter's stubborn adherence to motherhood as the routine of everyday nursing – of the type discussed earlier in the various versions of the myth of Demeter – sheds light on Yerma's obsession with motherhood. Yerma desires a child so that she can be absorbed in the daily tasks of upbringing, and thus distract her mind from her real problem which is the loss of her sexual and, eventually, personal identity.[50]

Greenfield (1981, 19) argues that this loss of individual integrity is central to the play and it is perfectly manifested in the climactic point of

[50] If Yerma had born a child it is likely that, finding fulfillment in the absorbing mother-child relationship, she would never have realized or resented the emptiness of her relationship with her husband. (Macpherson 1987, 38)

Juan's murder by Yerma when he looks at her "as you sometimes want a pigeon to eat." (ibid., 331)[51]

Yerma's frustration and anger over her sterility echoes Demeter's bitterness, her χολός over the loss of Persephone. It is with bitterness that Yerma cries: "I wish I were a woman." (Yerma 1976, 295) Her χολός is particularly evident in her discussion with Juan where she often becomes aggressive. It is also manifested in her bitter comments about herself and other women. When the Vieja tries to explain to her that marriage involves sexual attraction and pleasure because "So runs the world," Yerma responds in an embittered and angry manner: "Your world, but not mine". (ibid., 289) Like Demeter, Yerma becomes gradually more obsessed with the idea of possessing a child and in the end she becomes this "frenzied maenad" of the Homeric hymn. It is not her sterility that enrages her but her unfulfilled self, her sexually dry existence which she wants to redeem through motherhood. Arturo Barea calls her "a possessed priestess of maternity." (Barea 1994, 39) She is as possessed as a maenad, as frenzied as Demeter when she rushes through the forests to meet Persephone.

It is with deep anger, with this "dog-like" anger, that she chokes her husband to death. While in Tennyson and the Homeric hymn, Demeter afflicts the Olympians – arguably responsible for the loss of her daughter – Yerma punishes Juan not merely because she holds him responsible for her childlessness but, most importantly, because she also holds him responsible for her unfulfilled sexual life.

At this point, Yerma's sexual frustration becomes even more evident as the dramatic progression of the play reveals her fallacy. She has created a notion of motherhood according to her own standards (as shown in the scene with Maria) and she has desperately clung to it as her only salvation. Like Demeter, she sees motherhood as an anchor and a lifesaver, and has resorted to the self-conviction that possession of a child equals happiness whereas absence of child equals misery and desolation. Virtual motherhood is the consolation for this miserable state.

The question that inevitably arises is why these two women choose to have such an attitude towards motherhood. As far as Demeter is concerned, there is almost no evidence as to why she is so much attached to the idea of possessing and nursing Persephone. The original myth about her – the Homeric hymn – does not provide any details of their relationship because a hymn by nature is not supposed to dwell on such particularities but rather

[51] Greenfield (1981, 18-21) looks at the character of Yerma in relation to the dramatic development of the play and argues that this absolute annulment of Yerma's individual integrity which culminates in the end, constitutes the "climactic *coupe de grâce*" of the play.

focus on the praise of the person for whom it is being written. The only suggestion of Demeter's possessive and needy personality are her reactions after Persephone's abduction. Dove's version is, in fact, explicitly suggesting what can only be inferred from the Homeric hymn, namely that Demeter depends on Persephone and not Persephone on Demeter as it would be assumed. As far as Yerma is concerned, she has constructed a fallacious notion of motherhood in order to cope with her own sexual frustration. In other words, she has unconsciously created the belief that the daily routine of nursing and the suffering it involves (according to her) will redeem her from the state of confusion that she is experiencing. Yerma does not admit her need for sexual fulfilment because she thinks that seeking it is sinful or "inappropriate" and in order to cleanse herself from this guilt she seeks the pure and "appropriate" experience of motherhood. This also enables her to be in tune with the morality of contemporary Andalusian Catholicism, which views copulation as a means of procreation.

"I wish I were a woman" (Lorca 1976, 295): this phrase epitomizes Yerma's loss of identity. Not only is she unable to fulfil the social/religious role of a woman by becoming a mother but she is totally incapable of experiencing even the slightest epidermic sensation. Motherhood then becomes for her an anchor, an alibi for her lost sexuality and a final hope for a meaningful marriage and a justified existence as a woman. Her desperate calls to Juan for a child within their marriage are nothing but a disguised call for a mutually fulfilling marital life.

The fallacy inherent in Demetrian motherhood also pertains to Yerma's notion of motherhood. The child is a means of compensating for the lack of identity and personal fulfilment. Ironically, both Demeter and Yerma have been established as the symbols of true, selfless motherhood and the power of maternal instinct. In this Chapter I have shown that both of them communicate a fallacious notion of motherhood which acts as a compensation for an incomplete existence. Yerma's rejection of Juan facilitates the understanding of her obsession with a child and is therefore an essential part of the discussion of her character. The Demetrian rage and frustration over the loss of Persephone sheds light on Yerma as an equally enraged and frustrated virtual mother and her character operates as a reflection of Demetrian fallacious motherhood.

CHAPTER THREE

REINSTATING *THE GREAT CHIMERA*: *ἜΡΩΣ* DENIED, OR THE PREDICAMENT OF FEMALE PASSION

The Great Chimera has been characterized as one of Karagatsis's "sexual" works, and as one of his most representative novels (Meraklis 1981, 53) "permeated by lust and by sensuality which are the driving forces" (Haris 1981, 203). The author himself still bears the label of the "sexual" writer of the Generation of the thirties in Modern Greek literature.[52] His preoccupation with sexuality has further earned him the title *ἐρωτοσαρκικός* (erotofleshly) (Karouzos 1981, 47).[53] It has been pointed out that Karagatsean heroes are fundamentally "homines erotici" (Mitsakis 1977, 100) destroyed by hedonistic passion (Glezos 1981, 29) and that his stories are characterized by an almost obsessive sexual disposition (ibid.) and a veneration of lust (*ἡδονολατρεία*) (Karantonis 1977, 124)[54]. While critical consensus points to a Karagatsean notion of passion as a strictly libidinal urge, Karagatsis himself attributed this preoccupation to his task as a novelist which involves the representation of ordinary, average people and their daily concerns, one of them being erotic desire. The author acknowledged unreservedly the significance of sexuality and through his work he articulated the role it plays in everyday life. In a rare interview that he gave in 1949, when asked to comment on the ease with which he refers to sexuality, his response was

---

[52] The term "Generation of the Thirties" refers to Greek authors who appeared in modern Greek belles lettres during the decade of the 1930s. Their main characteristics were their attempt to break with the traditional literary scene by introducing elements of naturalism, realism and modernism as well as their preoccupation with the aftermath of the Asia Minor catastrophe. "The new writers turned their eyes to broader horizons, tried to trace more complicated psychological conditions, and to face more serious social and human problems, and also to cross the narrow limits of Hellenism while making an advanced parallel with that of European prose." (Politis 1973, 247)

[53] This qualifier was in fact coined by the poet Nikos Karouzos in an attempt to register Karagatsis's concern with sex and sexuality.

[54] Translations from Meraklis, Haris, Karouzos, Glezos and Karantonis are my own.

one of amazement and surprise at the idea that his sexual references were considered to be in any way unnatural.[55]

Undoubtedly, sexuality is of paramount importance in Karagatsis's oeuvre not only thematically but also narratologically, and in *The Great Chimera* it is one of the main axes around which the narrative revolves. Nonetheless, apprehending Karagatsean Ἔρως as nothing more than libidinal urge constitutes not only a misinterpretation of the whole novel but furthermore a reductive evaluation of the heroine as a sexually obsessed woman.[56] *The Great Chimera* is not simply a "sexual work" of Karagatsis's but a sophisticated inquiry into the dynamics of female passion.[57] This Chapter entertains the argument that the passion which Marina, the heroine of the novel, feels for her brother-in-law consists of more than a casual sexual attraction and transcends the limits of a typical infatuation constituting a powerful amalgamation of sexual, emotional and intellectual

---

[55] His actual response was: "Why? What is strange about it?" (Terencio 1993, 84) The following part of the interview reveals even more about his liberal approach to sexuality which was considered offensive and even obscene by readers and critics of the 1940s and 1950s.

Y.T.: Well, this is strange to the reader, who is not used either to talk or to read about these things, so openly.

M.K.: I find this a pseudo-puritanism. Is there anything more natural than two civilized people talking about these matters, the daily matters. Why should we describe what the hero eats and where he goes and not describe these reactions of his, which are as natural as his eating?

Y.T.: Yes, but I think that there is the impression that you don't talk as much about the food he eats, as you do about what he does in his sexual affairs. In other words, it is as if you give primary importance to this issue; as if it concerns you a lot.

M.K.: Yes, it does concern me a lot, like all of us, but I have the courage to admit it. With regard to its significance in my books, I don't think that it is greater than what's necessary. I simply place the issue within the suitable context; I give to it the same position that it has in life.

Y.T.: It is sincerity then that motivates you and not a tendency to be provocative.

M.K.: That's right. Besides I do not exaggerate neither do I describe details. But I also don't use evasive words in order to hide normal situations which are usually either insinuated or omitted out of puritanism. (ibid., 85-86. My translation)

[56] As a result of this misapprehension the novel has been considered a forbidden book for decades and was severely criticized by contemporary Athenian bourgeoisie, particularly by female readers.

[57] Karagatsis had an extensive familiarity with Freudian theories and in his works he emphasizes the power of libido and the significance of childhood experiences on sexuality and sexual behaviour. In *The Great Chimera*, for example, there is a great emphasis on the sexual licentiousness of Marina's mother as opposed to the austere, puritanical nature of her father and the eventual impact of these two figures on Marina's sexuality.

allure which, even when sexually consummated, is denied to the heroine, and to which death becomes the only resolution.

The Chapter looks at three different versions of the myth of Phaedra, a woman tormented by erotic passion for her stepson, with the objective of exploring female passion in its various guises, considering different reactions to it and concluding with a discussion of suicide as the only resolution to such an unrealizable passion. The fundamental myth that is distilled out of these three versions is that of a comprehensive and absolute passion which leads to suicide as an act of liberation. This fundamental myth of the impossible passion is subsequently applied to a reading of the character of Marina and exposes the chimerical nature of her passion (typified and manifested in the very title of the novel) in order to reinstate *The Great Chimera* as a novel about Ἔρως. For the purposes of this Chapter Ἔρως capitalized is understood as a profound sexual, intellectual and spiritual connection.

The three versions of the myth concerning Phaedra are Euripides's *Hippolytus*, Jean Racine's *Phèdre* and Yael Lotan's novel *Phaedra.* The Euripidean tragedy presents a rigid heroine with intense feelings and solid moral codes which dictate her choice to deny her feelings and her subsequent death. Passion here connotes a lust consistently resisted by the heroine and it is presented as deviance, in accordance with the Classical Greek cultural and social mores. Racine's play appropriates the same concept to the Christian ideology of love, and renders it as a cerebral passion while exposing the mental state of the heroine as a vacillation between a denial and an acceptance of her passion, highlighting thus the atrocity and injustice of her death in the end.[58] Lotan's twentieth-century version presents an intimate and emotion-oriented passion with spiritual nuances to which the heroine succumbs immediately.

[58] The relationship between Racine's plays and Christian theosophy, as suggested in Jansenism, is not addressed in my discussion of Racine as it does not relate to the argument regarding Racine's representation of female passion.

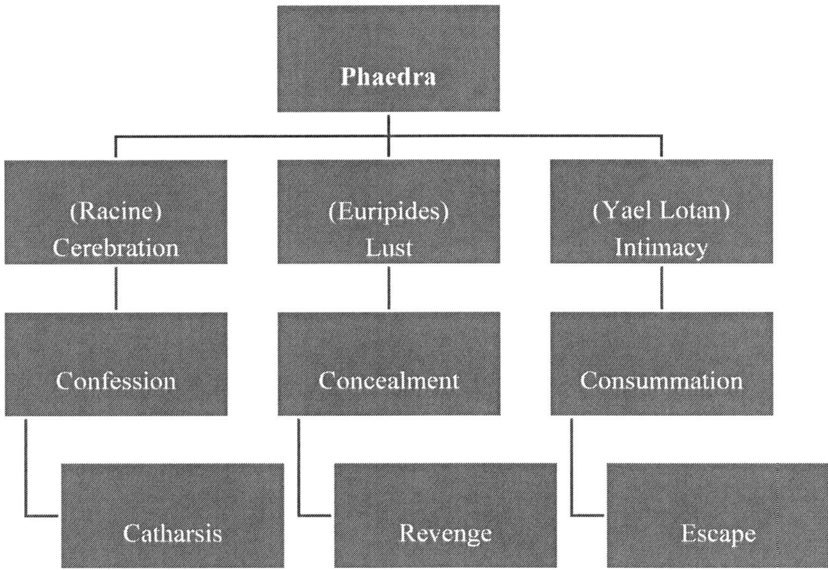

The following pages provide a comparative exploration of the three pivotal components in the presentation of the heroine's passion in the three versions of the myth: female passion in its various guises, the reactions of the heroine to it and the significance of the act of suicide as a common conclusion to all three versions. This exploration eventually reveals a comprehensive and unrealizable female passion.

Euripides's play is titled *Hippolytus*, suggesting that the focus of the tragedy is not on Phaedra but on her stepson. Indeed, Phaedra's presence in the play is rather brief and great emphasis is placed on Hippolytus's chastity and innocence. Nonetheless, her significance does not lie in her quantitative presence in the tragedy but in her qualitative and dramatic role. According to Peter Arnott (1977, 81) Euripides's original conception involved equally divided dramatic interest between Phaedra and Hippolytus as the epitomes of two antithetical states, passion and chastity. Eventually Phaedra became the protagonist of the play leaving Hippolytus a secondary, though not insignificant, role in the tragedy. In Arnott's own words

> The balance is not equal, and Phaedra steals the show. Our sympathy is much more likely to go to a woman devoured by passion against her will than to a

> youth who seems frigid, self-satisfied and inhumanly unresponsive to the needs of others. Even in the author's lifetime his public was beginning to refer to the play as *Phaedra*, rather than by its given title. (ibid., 81-82)[59]

The overall predominance of Phaedra, manifested in the constant engagement of scholars, critics, poets and authors with her character, and the abundance of critical discussion, artistic works and theatrical adaptations that she has inspired, suggests an emphatic preoccupation with female passion.

In this original myth of Phaedra, the heroine experiences a profound and powerful lust which agitates her physically as well as mentally and which she is determined to subdue. In the opening scene of the play the goddess Aphrodite declares that upon seeing Hippolytus Phaedra's heart was overwhelmed by a "dreadful longing":

> ἐλθόντα γάρ νιν Πιτθέως ποτ' ἐκ δόμων
> σεμνῶν ἐς ὄψιν καὶ τέλη μυστηρίων
> Πανδίονος γῆν πατρὸς εὐγενὴς δάμαρ
> ἰδοῦσα Φαίδρα καρδίαν κατέσχετο
> ἔρωτι δεινῷ τοῖς ἐμοῖς βουλεύμασιν.
> (Euripides 1995, 126)

> One day when he came from Pittheus' house to the land of Pandion to witness and perform the august Mysteries, his father's high-born wife Phaedra saw him, and her heart was seized with a dreadful longing: this was my devising. (ibid., 127)

The word ἔρωτι registers longing but it also suggests a more refined attraction as it is chosen over the word ἵμερος which denotes procreative lust. The adjective δεινῷ, "dreadful" which means fearful, terrible, dire clearly suggests catastrophe and misfortune foreshadowing, thus, the subsequent tragedy, and indicating the wicked nature of Phaedra's attraction to Hippolytus. David Kovacs's translation of the word δεινῷ, as "dreadful" captures the nuances of the word in the original text as it suggests affliction and peril while underscoring the unnaturalness of the heroine's feelings for young Hippolytus and her own sense of terror upon realizing her incestuous lust. The verb κατέσχετο (was seized) indicates the abrupt, powerful and violent act of Phaedra's falling in love with Hippolytus and points to a seizure, a violent attack, a possession. Τοῖς ἐμοῖς βουλεύμασιν (this was my devising) is an articulation of the deterministic predicate which annuls

---

[59] Phaedra indeed steals the show not only in performance, as Arnott argues, but even in a mere reading of the play: her lines, though much fewer in number than Hippolytus's, are so concise and so effective at rendering her passion that the overall effect is the dramatic predominance of her character and her struggle.

human freedom and renders man a puppet in the hands of the gods. The heroine's passion therefore is rendered from the very beginning of the play as a powerful, malevolent and potentially dangerous condition.

This "dreadful longing" that Phaedra feels for Hippolytus is undoubtedly sexual attraction and lust. Admittedly, she is in a state of a frenzied infatuation: "ἐμάνην, ἔπεσον δαίμονος ἄτῃ" (ibid., 146) (I was mad, I fell, and it was the doing of some divinity) (ibid., 147). The word ἐμάνην, past tense of the verb μαίνομαι, which is the root of the words mania and Maenad, points to the rage and agitation of the heroine, while ἄτῃ indicates the sexual nature of this agitation and suggests infatuation. The word δαίμονος is not only an affirmation of the divine involvement in the play, as this is specified in the introductory soliloquy of the goddess,[60] but it further establishes the violent and powerful seizure (κατέσχετο) that the heroine experiences. Ruth Padel (1995, 57) argues that δαίμων is more than a divine or supernatural impulse; it is an invasion, an aggressive, malevolent attack on humans by gods:

> In all cultures, images of disease interact with other available images of how you feel hurt. In Greece, the core of these is invasion: a central image also in the experience of divinity. Disease, like pollution and passion, is part of the "coming-in things" by which Hippocratics explain how people sicken. Intrusion, armed attack, is also how daimon gets back to work on you, in you.

In the case of Phaedra, δαίμων consists of a diseased emotion constituting a peculiar inner miasma (Kovacs 1987, 45): "Χεῖρες μὲν ἁγναί, φρὴν δ' ἔχει μίασμά τι" (Euripides 1995, 154) (My hands are clean. It is my heart that's stained) (ibid., 155). This δαίμων involves a diseased mind manifesting itself in mental deviation and self-alienation:"ποῖ παρεπλάγχθην γνώμης ἀγαθῆς;" (ibid., 146)[61] (Where have I wandered from the path of good sense?) (ibid., 147) In *Hippolytus,* therefore, passion as lust connotes insanity and mental instability. The word φρὴν and its derivatives are repeatedly mentioned in the play: "ἀφροσύνας" (ibid., 138), "παράφρων"

[60] In Classical Greece δαίμων was used for any kind of deity or supernatural power, whether of a benign or malicious nature. The only difference between a δαίμων and a god (θεὸς) was that a δαίμων was of a lesser grandeur and stature.

[61] Ruth Padel (1995, 120-164) offers an informative discussion on this mental deviation or as she calls it "inner wandering" which appears often in Classical Greek literature and writings. Interestingly enough when she discusses verbs with the prefix παρα which connote a mental deflection, she does not include the verb παραπλάζω used by Phaedra in its passive past tense, παρεπλάγχθην. The verb actually means to drive, to wander from the right way.

(ibid., 144), "φρονοῦσα" (ibid., 152), "φρὴν δ'ἔχει μίασμά τι" (ibid., 154), "σώφρονες" (ibid., 160), "εὖ φρονεῖν" (ibid., 162 and 212), "εὖ φρενῶν" (ibid., 168), "κακῶν φρενῶν" (ibid.) "ἡ δὲ φρήν ἀνώμοτος" (ibid., 184). The word φρὴν denotes the seat of the mental faculties as well as of emotional reactions. The distinction between good and bad φρὴν implies a neutral signification of the word; φρὴν itself possesses neither a positive nor a negative meaning. Passion is the malfunction of φρὴν, the loss of εὖ φρονεῖν. Passion in this play amounts to lust and is always referred to as ἔρως, ἐρᾶν, πόθος. The Classical Greek notion of reason corresponds to the proper functioning of one's φρένες and to "the Athenian male upper-class ideal of 'self'-control whose inner correlative is an unruffled phrēn." (Padel 1995, 128)[62] The opposite state, that of the loss or malfunction of φρὴν, is the state of mental instability and madness which is the "extreme of tragic passion." (ibid., 164) This malfunction of εὖ φρονεῖν which is inflicted upon the female protagonist and is contrasted with the male-attributed self-control and reason, enhances the apprehension of female passion as deviant and diseased and hence a terrible, destructive (δεινῷ), supernatural (δαίμονος) and manic (ἐμάνην) condition. It is precisely this apprehension of female passion as deviance and abnormality which accounts for the fact that it is eventually denied to the heroine, and it is also found, in a subtler form, in the transformed versions of the original myth.

Tragedy as a genre is most appropriate for the expression of strong passions and inner conflicts. "Tragedy specializes in this state: people who are aphrōn, 'phren-less', 'empty of phrenes', or 'stupid', 'insane.'" (ibid., 128) Dramatic characterization and verse foster the representation of the conflict inherent in the binary of passion and reason while dialogues, soliloquies and monologues are most effective channels of the underlying tensions.

The consequences of this inner disease include the heroine's affliction by an external, physical disease. The chorus informs us that "she lies afflicted, they say, on a bed of sickness" (Euripides 1995, 137), suggesting a gradual deterioration of her physical state. She is physically frail and unable to perform simple daily tasks: "Raise my body, hold my head erect! My limbs are unstrung! Take my fair arms, servants! It is a burden to have this headdress on my head. Take it off, spread my tresses on my shoulders!" (ibid., 143) This physical deterioration is confirmed by the chorus who remarks: "How weak and wasted her body is!" (ibid., 149)

---

[62] It is very important here to point out the distinction between reason as φρὴν, coinciding with the Western ratio which is associated with authority, and Classical Greek λόγος which is the exercise of free, individual thinking and is not necessarily contradictory to ἔρως but on the contrary may be seen as complementary to it.

Euripides places this struggle within a macrocosmic context through the employment of Aphrodite and Artemis. The divine binary manifests the opposition between lust and celibacy, between an excess of Ἔρως on the one hand and a complete lack of it on the other. This opposition subsequently represents the conflict between Ἔρως as excess, and celibacy as moderation, in accordance with the Classical Greek discourse of reason as sanity and passion as deviation. This symbolic representation, which is an appropriation of an inner conflict to the socio-cultural framework of Classical Greece, is not only a concise rendition of this conflict but it further illustrates the supremacy of Ἔρως over reason in the success of Aphrodite's project and the failure of Artemis to interfere with it.

Phaedra's reference to her mother's affair with the bull, leaves no doubt as to the lustful and inappropriate nature of her attraction to her stepson, yet at the same time it partly accounts for it since Phaedra has inherited her lustful nature from her mother:[63] "Ὦ τλῆμον, οἷον, μῆτερ, ἠράσθης ἔρον." (Euripides 1995, 156) (Unhappy mother, what a love was yours!) (ibid., 157)[64] Pasiphae's lust for the bull was both inappropriate and destructive. Once again female passion is identified with deviance, transgression and abnormality.

In this original myth of Phaedra, Euripides is more sympathetic towards his heroine and attributes her wickedness to δαίμων. He therefore succeeds in making her both the villain and the heroine of the tragedy. Furthermore, in his version, Phaedra realizes her own state of self-alienation and the inappropriate nature of her feelings for Hippolytus, and this realization and the sense of guilt that she experiences render her even more appealing to the audience.

In short, Phaedra's lust is an intense and powerful infatuation, the result of divine affliction as well as inherited perversion.[65] The intensity and

---

[63] Phaedra's mother Pasiphae, was the wife of the King of Crete Minos. Pasiphae experienced an infatuation for a bull and the result of this miscegenation was the birth of the Minotaur, a creature which was half human and half bull.

[64] Apart from the noun ἔρον, the verb ἠράσθης, which is the past tense of ἔρωμαι and has as its root the word ἔρως, enhances the sexual nature of Pasiphae's attraction to the bull.

[65] Webster (1967, 64-76) refers to fragments from an earlier version of the play which have survived, and they indicate a different treatment of Phaedra and her lust for Hippolytus by Euripides. This first version is titled *Hippolytus Kalyptomenos* (*Hippolytus Covered*) because Hippolytus covered his head in order not to be polluted by Phaedra's incestuous and tainted impulses. In this play, Webster argues, Euripides is less sympathetic towards Phaedra and presents her as a woman who "offers herself to a younger man." (ibid., 65) Kitto (1993, 205-206) also points out that the first version of *Hippolytus* portrays Phaedra as a perverted, vicious woman

power of this lustful passion, manifested in the severe mental and physical affliction that the heroine experiences, affirm the catalytic effect of Ἔρως upon the human predicament, but most significantly the representation of female passion as devious and potentially destructive.

In Racine's play, Phèdre's attraction to Hippolyte is more complex as her passion is cerebral and gravitates towards a christianized love (amour, as opposed to the Classical Greek ἔρως) and hence in accordance with the stylization prevalent in classical French drama; Racinian theatre is essentially "psychological drama" (de Mourges 1967, 37) and attempts to establish a new insight into human nature by shifting the emphasis onto the mental processes of the protagonist. This christianized and humanized perspective results in a mitigation of the rendition of female passion as deviant and abnormal, but at the same time it underscores the cruelty of the heroine's death by creating a contrast between her human struggle and the inhuman outcome.

In entitling his play *Phèdre,* Racine shifts the focus formally to the character of Phèdre while proclaiming a conscious preoccupation with female passion. Upon her very first appearance on stage the Racinian Phèdre resembles the Euripidean Phaedra. Her attraction to Hippolyte is presented as a divine attack and as an unwanted mental disease inflicted upon her by an external force. To her nurse Oenone it is an unidentified illness and she refers to it as a "hidden malady", an "eternal discord" and a "restless anguish" that "reigns within her mind" (Racine 1970, 154). Phèdre herself though is conscious of the mental implications of her condition and refers to it as an insanity: "Madness! Where am I, what have I said? Whither have my desires, my reason strayed? Lost, lost the gods have carried it away." (Racine 1970, 156) Fully aware of the moral implications of this madness, she apprehends it as a miasma. Not only has her "reason strayed" but it has also been substituted by unnatural, tainted thoughts and desires: "my hands have done no wrong. Would God my heart were innocent as they!" (ibid., 158) Finally she declares that this madness, this miasma relates to love: "Love's furies rage in me" (ibid., 160) insinuating the passion for her stepson.

Nonetheless, Phèdre's symptoms are not those of the typical infatuation of the manner that was illustrated in Euripides's *Hippolytus*; her symptoms rather constitute an obsession, an emotional and mental fixation, a cerebral passion.

---

and therefore deprives the play of its wider metaphysical and philosophical foundation, namely, that lust and inappropriate sexual attraction are a potential in all human beings.

J'adorais Hippolyte ; et le voyant sans cesse,
Même au pied des autels que je faisais fumer,
J'offrais tout à ce dieu que je n'osais nommer.
Je l'evitais partout. Ô comble de misère!
Mes yeux le retrouvaient dans les traits de son père.
(Racine 1980, 590)

I worshipped him. His image followed me.
Even on the altar's steps, my offerings
Were only to the god I dared not name.
I shunned him everywhere. O crowning woe!
I found him mirrored in his father's face!
(Racine 1970, 161)

The Euripidean text contains only a brief and rather vague reference to the temple built by Phaedra ostensibly for Aphrodite but in fact for Hippolytus and which was later named after him: "Before she came to this land of Troizen she built, next to the rock of Pallas, a temple to Cypris overlooking this land since she loved a foreign love. After ages shall name the goddess's shrine for Hippolytus." (Euripides 1995, 127) The Racinian text however presents an account of Phèdre's own experience in the temple while she literally worships her beloved, providing thus an insight into her mental state and illustrating the nature and depth of her passion for him. The Racinian heroine is obsessed with Hippolyte and not only does she fantasize about him constantly but the power of this fantasy is so strong that it cannot be subdued even temporarily for the purposes of a religious worship; "Even when my lips invoked the goddess' name, I worshipped him." (ibid.) The culmination of this effect, registered in the words *voyant* and *yeux*, is the mental fusion of father and son; "I found him mirrored in his father's face!" (ibid.)

The fusion of Hippolyte and Theseus that takes place in Phèdre's mind is illustrated in her confession to Hippolyte and provides further insight into her mental state via the articulation of her inner, subjective voice.

Oui, Prince, je languis, je brûle pour Thésée.
Je l'aime, non point tel que l'ont vu les enfers,
Volage adorateur de mille objets divers,
Qui va du dieu des morts déshonorer la couche,
Mais fidèle, mais fier, et même un peu farouche,
Charmant, jeune, traînant tous les coeurs après soi,
Tel qu'on dépeint nos dieux, ou tel que je vous voi.
Il avait votre port, vos yeux, votre langage,
Cette noble pudeur colorait son visage.
(Racine 1980, 600-601)

> Yes, Prince, I pine, I am on fire for him.
> I love King Theseus, not as once he was,
> the fickle worshipper at countless shrines,
> dishonouring the couch of Hades' god;
> but constant, proud, and even a little shy;
> enchanting, young, the darling of all hearts,
> fair as the gods; or fair as you are now.
> He had your eyes, your bearing, your speech.
> His face flushed with your noble modesty.
> (Racine 1970, 175)

This powerful, emotional soliloquy reveals the nature and intensity of the heroine's passion. The words "pine" and "on fire", placed in the first line of her soliloquy, not only indicate the degree of her passion but they also affirm the fanciful manner in which she experiences this passion. In the original je languis conveys the sense of melting, disintegration, which renders the state of psychological and physical torment that Phèdre is in. Unlike the Euripidean representation of a lustful, possessed (ἔπεσον δαίμονος αἴσῃ) and manic (ἐμάνην) heroine, Racine portrays an altogether different Phèdre whose agitation is far from the manic state demonstrated in the Euripidean text. His Phèdre does not suffer from a typical infatuation of a mature woman for a younger man, as the Euripidean play allows us to assume, but is attracted to a particular mental construct, a Gestalt that her own mind has produced and which is a hybrid created out of the fusion of Theseus and Hippolyte. Her passion, therefore, is a distillation of a mental process in which father and son are amalgamated into an unidentified lover.

This imaginary lover has Hippolyte's eyes, his demeanour, his speech and his noble modesty. He is enchanting, young and fair as the gods. He also has Hippolyte's virtuous character: constant, proud, shy and enchanting, qualities which contrast greatly with the fickle and dishonouring Theseus. Due to the cerebral nature of her passion, Phèdre is drawn to particular qualities of this fictitious lover, pertaining mainly to his character and his personality. She is attracted to his integrity (constant), his humility (noble modesty, even a little shy), his pride. In her mind he represents a more refined and ameliorated version of the brutal and promiscuous Theseus and, in that sense, the impropriety of her attraction to Hippolyte is not only mitigated but even becomes legitimized.

This cerebral passion becomes more pronounced through the transformation of Phèdre's confession into a living fantasy during which the original incident of Ariadne's offer of assistance to Theseus in the Labyrinth is reconstructed and converted into an encounter between Phèdre and Hippolyte.

> Ma soeur du fil fatal eût armé votre main.
> Mais non, dans ce dessein, je l'aurais devancée.
> L'amour m'en eût d'abord inspiré la pensée ;
> C'est moi, Prince, c'est moi, dont l'utile secours
> Vous eût du Labyrinthe enseigné les détours.
> Que de soins m'eût coûtés cette tête charmante!
> Un fils n'eût point assez rassuré votre amante:
> Compagne du péril qu'il vous fallait chercher,
> Moi-même devant vous j'aurais voulu marcher,
> Et Phèdre au labyrinthe avec vous descendue
> Se serait avec vous retrouvée ou perdue.
> (Racine 1980, 601)

> My sister would have armed you with the thread
> To lead you through the dark entangled maze –
> No. I would have forestalled her. For my love
> Would instantly have fired me with the thought.
> I, only I, would have revealed to you
> The subtle windings of the labyrinth.
> What care I would have lavished on your head!
> A thread would not have reassured my fears.
> Affronting danger side by side with you,
> I would myself have wished to lead the way,
> And Phaedra, with you in the labyrinth,
> Would have returned with you or met her doom.
> (Racine 1970, 175-176)

Indeed, one of the most significant images in the play is the Labyrinth which metaphorizes the intricacy of Phèdre's passion. Its complexity is emblematic of her own sense of confusion and entrapment, and it further signifies her sense of disorientation and abandonment. In a sense it metaphorizes her own experience of articulating her passion to Hippolyte; her speech, which sets out as a plea for her children's life, operates as a mental and linguistic maze in which she finds herself trapped, unable to retreat, subjected to a trajectory that will most certainly lead her to meet her doom. It is a "vision that lures her to total surrender, from a dream shaped out of her words, borne on the sinuous lines of the speech." (Vinaver 1969, 156)

The metaphoricity of the Labyrinth in combination with the imagistic quality of Phèdre's hallucinatory aveu are, according to Roland Barthes, (1964, 17-20) part of the Racinian erotic rhetoric, where the birth of love is recalled in the form of a trance or a dream and becomes what he calls the Racinian "erotic scene" which enacts "the most vital but also the most fragile moment of the conflict." (ibid., 21) Indeed, the scene in the Labyrinth is a stylized externalization of the heroine's innermost desires. The use of the third person (et Phèdre) suggests frustration as well as a blurred identity as Phèdre is both the author and the protagonist of this imaginary scene.

Furthermore, the reference to the Labyrinth reflects the first Racinian principle of "interiority" or "intimacy" of the central action[66] according to which the real action takes place in the psyche of the main character (Weinberg 1963, 256). The use of the Labyrinth facilitates the stylized externalization of the heroine's state of mind as this develops throughout her confession. The very topography of the Labyrinth suggests an abolition of differences in the characters, and functions as a paradigm of the total surrender to passion (Lepine 1994, 47-62).

Hence, in an interesting twist to the Aristotelian notion of tragedy as the imitation of a grandiose and complete action, Racinian action is an internalized action, and tragedy therefore becomes mimetic of an intimate, private pathos:

> Even when he depicts characters who are by the standards of almost any age lost souls, devoured by ugly passions and reckless self-gratification, he somehow sees them from inside and makes us enter into their inner selves, when they might otherwise horrify and appal us. (Bowra 1969, 40)

This inner self of Phèdre that Racine presents us with is hardly horrific or appalling; on the contrary through the exposition of her thoughts and mental meanderings she is rendered more human and fallible, and the entirety of Act II becomes, in fact, "a portrait of the passionate being" (Lee 1996, 88). Through the use of dramatic monologue, which functions not merely as a rhetorical device but also as a vehicle for subjectivity, Racine eventually achieves a transformation of female passion from an irrational and manic state to a subtle and cerebral experience.

In short, the Racinian version of the myth of Phaedra presents a stylized and refined passion, transforming the heroine of the myth from the lustful Maenad of antiquity into the seventeenth-century cerebral lover under the sway of a more legitimate passion which is, nonetheless, denied to her.

---

[66] According to Bernard Weinberg (1963, 255-297), Racine's work is permeated by three principles which underlie the dramatic development of his plays. The first principle is the principle of "interiority" or "intimacy" of the central action, or in other words the placement of the action in the mind and psyche of the protagonist rather than in external events and incidents. The second principle is that of the "subordination of all secondary actions and episodes to the main action", and the third principle is that of "the meticulous provision and the full realization of probabilities for every event in the action."

In Yael Lotan's version, passion consists primarily of a remarkable intimacy that the heroine feels for her stepson, to which she succumbs with no hesitation or remorse. Her Phaedra is overwhelmed by a sense of a strong emotional connection to her stepson, Alexis and this is, perhaps, the most significant element in her passion.

First and foremost, Phaedra shares her stepson's fervour for artistic and intellectual activities, having been involved herself, in her early youth, in such activities, which she eventually abandoned after her marriage to her tycoon husband, Thanos. Despite her wealthy background and the opulent and materialistic environment she was raised in, Phaedra is by nature attracted to artistic and creative activities: as a young student she had aspired to be a singer, while falling in love with a music professor. Her encounter with Alexis evokes these memories and becomes a reminder of an aspect of her personality and psyche to which she had been oblivious and which she was suppressing. Alexis's "preoccupation with the beautiful and the subtle" (Lotan 1962, 21), which contrasts strongly with the "crude and explicit force" (ibid.,) of his father, not only has a strong impact on her but also plays a pivotal role in her attraction to him.

This attraction is cemented by Alexis's imaginative and creative temperament which enchants Phaedra. While in the old attic of her Parisian house he begins to tell her an old story from the French Revolution and the manner of his narration stimulates her imagination and elicits powerful emotions in her.

> As Alexis spoke I could hear the clatter of the horse's hooves outside and the delicate and formal strains of a minuet down below. It was an elaborate and fantastic tale, but he managed to infuse an element of poetic truth into it, which, when he came to the terrible and tragic ending, made my eyes cloud over like a child's. (ibid., 39)

His unique creative charisma, manifested in his ability not only to create an "elaborate and fantastic tale" but also to "infuse an element of poetic truth in it", appeals to Phaedra's sensitivity and susceptibility to and appreciation of the subtleties involved in creativity. This experience that the two of them share, and the effect it has on the heroine, illustrates the mental and spiritual intimacy that she shares with her stepson.

Most significantly though, Phaedra experiences an immediate and profound emotional rapport with her stepson: "He was young and handsome, but he was not callow. He was almost reverent in his approach, yet so acutely perceptive that I felt sure he could hear my thoughts." (ibid., 37) This inner correspondence borders on the spiritual and the metaphysical: "I had never experienced such a strong sensation of intimacy with anyone, as though we had known each other for centuries and had been waiting to meet again." (ibid.)

This strong emotional bond is immediately manifested in their first full discussion in which Phaedra embarks on a conventional conversation between stepmother and stepson but eventually finds herself engaged in a revelatory monologue.

> I had meant to ask him many questions, about his school days and his family and friends. But instead, inspired perhaps by the gentle music and the nearness of the river, I found myself telling him about my own childhood and youth. He was closely attentive and from time to time made a simple remark which showed me he was in complete sympathy with my train of thought and wanted to follow it. I told him about our home, the grand old house with its shuttered darkness and vast, echoing, unused rooms. I told him about the rivalry between Ariadne and myself.
>
> Then I told him about Switzerland and the gentle and cultured young professor I fell in love with when I was seventeen. (ibid., 19)

The kind of affinity that she experiences with her stepson is something that she does not share with her husband. In her marriage she is confined to the role of a wife of a tycoon and she merely constitutes another one of his assets.

> On our seventh wedding anniversary Thanos gave me two presents: a ship – the SS Phaedra – and a beautiful diamond. The ship was beautiful – big and handsome, virile of power and feminine of line. It symbolised in my mind Thanos and me together. She bore my name and she belonged to him, and I thought it fit. (ibid., 1)

"Virile of power and feminine of line", these words encapsulate the dynamics of their marriage with power and action being attributed to masculinity while form and passivity to femininity. Phaedra's conviction that she "belongs" to her husband and is owned by him in the same manner as his entrepreneurial assets and material possessions, confirms the conventional and superficial nature of their relationship and contrasts with the freedom and profundity she experiences with Alexis. At the same time, it echoes the relationship of Phaedra and Theseus in the original myth where Phaedra is regarded as Theseus's trophy from Crete and is reduced to being the loyal wife awaiting her husband's return from his various adventures, in the same way that the twentieth-century Phaedra awaits Thanos's return from his long and distant business trips. However, Lotan's version of the myth provides a significant insight into the heroine's emotions and her intimate thoughts (accentuated by the first-person narrative) while revealing the loneliness that she experiences in her marriage. The effacement of her own identity within her marriage, juxtaposed to its rediscovery and redemption upon meeting Alexis, not only renders a much more human and appealing heroine (of the type portrayed in Racine's play) but it also justifies and, in a sense, compels her attraction to her stepson.

It is indeed noteworthy that the narrator is Phaedra herself and the story is told from her point of view. The whole novel is her "voice", her subjective self, reminiscent of the Voices/Stimmen in Christa Wolf's version of the myth of Medea, or the different points of view in Rita Dove's version of the myth of Demeter. Moreover, narration allows for the disclosure of intimate thoughts and feelings, provides a direct and clear insight into the heroine's mind, and is indicative of twentieth-century literary preoccupation with subjectivity and individuality.

The location of the first encounter between Alexis and his stepmother is the Elgin room of the British Museum. The Elgin Room is the equivalent of the Labyrinth in which the Racinian Phèdre fantasized about being trapped with Hippolyte. Unlike the Racinian Labyrinth however, the Elgin room is a spacious room and the semantics of the scene point to the realm of the metaphysical, which serves to accentuate the profound connection between the two of them. More particularly, the white marbles point to Classical antiquity, and hence to the original myth of Phaedra and Hippolytus, in conjunction with the struggle between reason and passion, while Alexis's drawing is an allusion to the artistic and the intellectual bond between himself and his stepmother. While the two other versions of the myth contain a brief reference to the first encounter between Phaedra and her stepson, in Lotan's version the narrative offers us a direct account of this first meeting and of the coupe de foudre as the heroine experiences it.

Alexis's fervour for his art and his defence of it becomes a reminder for Phaedra of her own similar dilemma when she was young, and enables her to discover a power within her to which she had been oblivious. Alexis's strength is inner, and his poetic manner of living life is some raison d'être which not only empowers Phaedra but also determines her attraction towards him.

The three versions of the myth of Phaedra present different facets of female passion and suggest an intense and agitating experience with a strong physical, mental and emotional impact which, through humanization, is transformed from a vicious and abnormal condition to a more legitimised one. While Euripides focuses on the potentially destructive qualities of female passion (ἔρωτι δεινῷ), Racine and Lotan focus on the mind and psyche of their heroines and therefore mitigate the Euripidean wickedness of female passion.

The reactions of the three heroines to the passion that overwhelms them, manifest the underlying inner conflict and determine the predicament of female passion.

The lustful Euripidean Phaedra is persistently trying to conceal her passion, consistent with the Classical Athenian decorum of αἰδώς, while the Racinian Phèdre engages in a series of confessions which set the plot in motion, in that they manifest her overall confusion in dealing with her cerebral passion, and the twentieth-century Phaedra proceeds with the consummation of her passion in the manner typical of the uninhibited modern woman.

The silence of the Euripidean Phaedra, dictated by the principles of αἰδώς and εὔκλεια,[67] enhances her tragic state as it highlights her struggle and elevates her to a tragic heroine. The beginning of the play establishes her resolution to remain silent. In the opening scene of the play it is announced by Aphrodite that Phaedra is slowly perishing in silence: ἀπόλλυται σιγῇ (Euripides 1995, 126)/"she means to die in silence" (ibid., 127), ξύνοιδε δ'οὔτις οἰκετῶν νόσον (ibid., 126)/"None of her household knows of her malady." (ibid., 127) Phaedra's own nurse declares her ignorance over her mistress's malady since she remains silent about it: πάντα γὰρ σιγᾷ τάδε (ibid., 148)/"on all these questions she is mute" (ibid., 149), κρύπτει γὰρ ἥδε πῆμα κοὔ φησιν νοσεῖν (ibid., 150)/"for she hides it and denies she's ill" (ibid., 150), οὐ μάντις εἰμὶ τ'αφανῆ γνῶναι σαφῶς (ibid., 158)/"I am no seer, to know for certain what's hidden." (ibid.,159)

This silence is not the result of a temperamental obstinacy but a part of a carefully processed plan: "ἠρξάμην μὲν οὖν ἐκ τοῦδε, σιγᾶν τήνδε καὶ κρύπτειν νόσον" (ibid., 162) (My starting point was this, to conceal my malady in silence" (ibid., 163)[68] Phaedra's "right mind" is consistent with the notion of αἰδώς and becomes more pronounced through the one-dimensional, obsessively celibate character of Hippolytus.[69] Her own αἰδώς is expressed explicitly: "κατ'ὄσσων δάκρυ μοι βαίνει, καὶ ἐπ'αἰσχύνην ὄμμα τέτραπται" (ibid., 146) (the tears stream down from my eyes and my gaze is turned to shame) (ibid., 147). She asks the Nurse to cover her head.

---

[67] Αἰδώς refers to the reticence that Athenian citizens had to display while εὔκλεια pertains to posthumous glory.

[68] Phaedra's plan consists of three stages: a) her decision to remain silent "for the tongue is not to be trusted" (Euripides 1995, 163), b) her intention to impose self-control as a means of overcoming her condition and c) her resolution to commit suicide in the event that the first two do not prove to be effective (ibid., 163-165).

[69] Luschnig (1983, 115-123) points out that Hippolytus's celibacy is a result not of restraint and self-discipline but of ignorance of passion and of any emotional/psychological pain.

Horror and shame are the feelings evoked by the mere naming of places and activities, such as forests and hunting, which by association involve Hippolytus: "αἰδούμεθα γὰρ τὰ λελεγμένα μοι" (ibid., 146) (I am ashamed of my words) (ibid., 147). Phaedra's sense of shame becomes pivotal as the whole play highlights the "anguish of passion" (Lesky 1965, 150). This anguish, is further emphasized through Hippolytus's obstinate adherence to celibacy which hardly qualifies him for the status of hero. Phaedra's persistent opposition to the passion incited by Aphrodite – manifested in her unwillingness to reveal her feelings – is a dramatic device on the part of Euripides, so that his heroine remains consistent to her silence and her virtue.[70]

Her reticence goes beyond a precaution against the impairment of her honour and εὔκλεια as she mentions in her monologue and indeed beyond what Rabinowitz (1987, 127-137) and Zeitlin (1996, 220) argue is an acknowledgement and acceptance of the misogynist Athenian ideology, which endorsed female passivity and silence.[71] Her choice to remain silent is in fact indicative of her wish to forget, not to know: "Τό γὰρ ὀρθοῦσθαι γνώμην ὀδυνᾶ, τό δέ μαινόμενον κακόν· ἀλλὰ κρατεῖ, μὴ γιγνώσκοντ'ἀπολέσθαι." (Euripides 1995, 146) (For to be right in my mind is grievous pain, while this madness is an ill thing. Best to perish in unconsciousness) (ibid., 147).

The concept of keeping silent, concealing, covering, permeates the play. The verb κρύπτω (hide) and its derivatives as well as the words σκιάζω (cast a shade), νέφος (cloud), καλύπτω (cover), σιγῶ (keep silent) appear regularly in the Euripidean text: "τειρομέναν νοσερᾷ κοίτᾳ δέμας ἐντὸς ἔχειν/οἴκων, λεπτά δε φά/ρη ξανθάν κεφαλὰν σκιάζειν" (ibid., 136) (She lies afflicted, they say, on a bed of sickness and keeps indoors, with fine-spun cloths shading her blond head) (ibid., 137), "στυγνόν δ' ὀφρύων νέφος

[70] In *Hippolytus Kalyptomenos*, Euripides had a scene in which Phaedra declared her love (in a similar manner to that of the Racinian Phèdre), yet in *Hippolytus* he omitted this scene and any confrontation between Phaedra and her stepson. Gilbert Murray (1913, 88) argues that by rewriting the play, Euripides "reached a far more austere and beautiful effect" and that "The story which might so easily be made ugly or sensual is treated by Euripides with a delicate and austere purity." (ibid., 89)

[71] According to Froma Zeitlin (1996, 220) Phaedra resorts to silence because she "knows too well the conventions of Greek social life that relegate the woman to a silence that would be her glory." Similarly, Nancy Sorkin Rabinowitz (1987, 130) contends that Phaedra "accepts what her misogynist culture and its misogynist representative Hippolytus say is appropriate for a woman, and seeks to suppress her desire, to die without speaking." (Rabinowitz 1987, 130) In her feminist reading of *Hippolytus* Rabinowitz argues that the play exemplifies the phallocentric Athenian culture which relegated women to silence and invisibility.

αυξάνεται" (ibid., 140) (The cloud of unhappiness on her brow is growing) (ibid., 141), "μαῖα, πάλιν μου κρύψον κεφαλήν" (ibid., 146) (Nurse, cover my head up again!) (ibid., 147), "κρύπτω τὸ δ'ἐμὸν πότε δὴ θάνατος/σῶμα καλύψει;" (ibid., 146) (I cover your head. But when will my body be covered in death?) (ibid., 147), "εἶέν, τί σιγᾷς; οὐκ ἐχρῆν σιγᾶν, τέκνον" (ibid., 150) (Well, why are you silent? You ought not to be silent, child) (ibid., 151), "κἄπειτα κρύπτεις, χρήσθ' ἱκνουμένης ἐμού;" (ibid., 156) (Why hide it? Then, when my request is noble?) (ibid., 157), "σιγῷμ'ἂν ἤδη" (ibid., 156) (I'll be silent) (ibid., 157)).

For Charles Segal, concealment is inextricably linked to the problem of human knowledge and the tragic vision of the destructive consequences of passion (Segal 1988, 263-282). This is articulated in the Nurse's first speech which suggests that concealment implies ignorance.

> πᾶς δ'ὀδυνηρὸς βίος ἀνθρώπων
> κοὐκ ἔστι πόνων ἀνάπαυσις.
> ἀλλ' ὅ τι τοῦ ζῆν φίλτερον ἄλλο
> σκότος ἀμπίσχων κρύπτει νεφέλαις.
> δυσέρωτες δὴ φαινόμεθ' ὄντες
> τοῦδ΄ὅ τι τοῦτο στίλβει κατὰ γῆν
> δι'ἀπειροσύνην ἄλλου βιότου
> κοὐκ ἀπόδειξιν τῶν ὑπό γαίας,
> μύθοις δ' ἄλλως φερόμεσθα.
> (Euripides 1995, 140-142)

> But the life of mortals is wholly trouble, and there is no rest from toil. Anything we might love more than life is hid in a surrounding cloud of darkness, and we show ourselves unhappy lovers of whatever light there is that shines on earth because we are ignorant of another life, and the world below is not revealed to us. We are aimlessly borne along by mere tales. (ibid., 141-143)

Placed at the beginning of the play this speech encapsulates perhaps the most significant notion underlying the actions both of Phaedra and Hippolytus. The latter represses his erotic self, remaining thus ignorant of love, sex, emotional suffering and of a whole part of his existence, while the former is in a state of denial regarding her passion. Both characters have a problematic relationship with truth and knowledge, and it is this very relationship that determines their predicament as *Hippolytus* is "a drama concerned with knowledge, with levels of knowing and not knowing, and with ways of knowing." (Luschnig 1988, 88)

The preoccupation with silence, concealment and the choice of not knowing, suggest once more an apprehension of female passion as shameful and inappropriate. This is accentuated through the figure of the sexually promiscuous Theseus who despite his constant infidelity and the disgraceful and "abnormal" act of fathering a child upon an Amazon, is beyond any criticism, and his notoriously lustful temperament is not considered improper or shameful.

While Euripides's Phaedra is determined not to reveal her vicious secret and is, overall, a rigid character, Racine's Phèdre appears highly frustrated at the revelation of her passion as she is presented in a more human and sympathetic way. Her frustration is manifested in her confessions – a Christian notion par excellence.

Unlike the Euripidean Phaedra who resorts to silence and only reveals her passion to her nurse forced by the custom of *ἱκεσία*,[72] Racine's heroine confesses her passion three times (to Oenone, to Hippolyte himself and in the end to Theseus) in a series of *aveux* which constitute the cornerstones upon which the play is constructed. (Turnell 1971, 243)

In the beginning of the play Racine's Phèdre appears very similar to Euripides's Phaedra, as she refuses to share her secret with her nurse and considers death as the most suitable solution. "I have revealed enough. Spare me the rest. I die, and my grim secret dies with me." (Racine 1970, 158) Racine retains the practice of ἱκεσία as a means of instigating Phèdre's confession to Oenone.[73]

Her second confession though is totally involuntary and takes the form "of a weakness, a lapsus, an unwitting revelation" (Weinberg 1963, 259). While pleading for her children's life she finds herself immersed in a genuine, revelatory monologue in which gradually "her passion overwhelms her, and social restraints are cast aside" (Arnott 1977, 89). The significance of this revelation pertains not only to Hippolyte's knowledge of her passion but, more significantly, to Phèdre's own self-knowledge. Contrary to the Euripidean Phaedra, Racine's Phèdre wishes to know and to let others know, to uncover, she chooses to be γιγνώσκουσα.

The third confession, which is a conscious, premeditated disclosure of the truth to Theseus, is indeed a Christian confession – Barthes in fact calls it a "correction" (Barthes 1964, 116) – as it restores truth and justice and elevates Phèdre spiritually. "It was I, Theseus, who on your virtuous, filial

---

[72] According to the custom of *ἱκεσία* if a person went down on their knees holding the other person's knee while making a request, the request could in no way be denied.

[73] Oenone: "By all the tears that I have shed for you,
And by your faltering knees I hold entwined,
Deliver me from dire uncertainty."
Phèdre: "You wish it. Rise" (Racine 1970, 159)

son made bold to cast a lewd, incestuous eye. Heaven in my heart lit an ill-omened fire. Detestable Oenone did the rest. (Racine 1970, 213)[74] As Roland Barthes argues, Phèdre's third confession is "literal, purified of all theatre; her language is totally coincident with fact, it is a correction: Phaedra can die, the tragedy is exhausted." (Barthes 1964, 116) It is a cathartic act, a choice of knowledge over ignorance, of truth over deception.

Phèdre's confessions are indicative of her oscillation between ignorance and knowledge, and she thus contrasts the Euripidean heroine who adheres consistently to silence and maintains ignorance of her condition. Racine creates a more human and genuine heroine who allows herself to be overwhelmed by her feelings of frustration and who eventually chooses truth and knowledge of herself and of her predicament.

Racinian heroes vacillate between impulse and mind or else between the desire to live, *vivre* and the need to restrain, *régner*. The Racinian view of life is that of a struggle between these two forces (Spoerri 1969, 57).[75] The notion of vivre in the Racinian discourse is the impulsive and emotion-oriented modus vivendi whereas the idea of régner refers to the submission of all emotions and impulses to reason. Spoerri contends that Racinian dialectics see the former as motion and chaos, and the latter as rest and stability:

> On the merely psychological plane the dichotomy *régner-vivre* confronts us in the counterpoint of rest-movement. Whereas the Romantic attaches value to movement, which means for him life, creative development, the flow of aspiration, while rest signifies on the other hand inhibition, rigidity and reserve, Racine emphasises rest as the positive factor; it means for him reassurance, taming, control, security, safety and clarity, in contrast to movement which is nothing other than obscure impulse, restlessness and confusion. The darkworld is the home of such concepts as trouble, *égarement, désordre, transport, agité*." (ibid., 56)

---

[74] Despite her ostensible dependence on Oenone, it is Phaedra herself, in fact, who makes the final choices and consents while Oenone is simply an instrument: "We realize then that *Phèdre* is also a tragedy of *accouchement*. Oenone is truly the nurse, the midwife, who seeks to liberate Phaedra from her words at any price, who "delivers" language from the deep cavity in which it is confined." (Barthes, 1964, 119).

[75] Spoerri borrows the terms from other plays by Racine, *Bérénice*, "Mais il ne s'agit plus de *vivre*, il faut *régner*" (4.5.1102) and *Bajazet*, 'Pour la dernière fois, veux-tu *vivre* et *régner*" (5.4.1540). According to Spoerri the tensions between *vivre* as impulse and *régner* as restraint constitute a pivotal axis around which Racinian heroes think and act.

This binary corresponds to the conflict between the μαινόμενον κακόν and the ὀρθοῦσθαι γνώμην which is posited in Euripides' play. In the Euripidean text however this conflict is bypassed through the alternative way of μὴ γιγνώσκοντ' ἀπολέσθαι. The struggle between these two antithetical states is indeed a fundamental one and determines the dynamics of both plays. As Pocock notes, *Phèdre*

> expresses with dreadful intensity the struggle between on the one hand violent and primitive passions and on the other the attempt to split them off from the self and deny them utterly. At the end, in varying degrees, the characters both have been destroyed by and have assimilated these passions. (Pocock 1973, 273-274)

In the Preface to the play, Racine refers to Phèdre as neither innocent nor guilty, suggesting therefore his own dilemma with respect not only to his heroine but to human nature as well: "Phèdre n'est ni tout a fait coupable, ni tout a fait innocente. Elle est engagée, par sa destinée et par la colère des dieux, dans une passion illégitime, dont elle a horreur toute la \première." (Racine 1980, 577) In that sense, as Butler points out, he is developing Euripides' concept of an evil passion by transforming the heroine of the original myth, and by assuming a sympathetic attitude towards her (Butler 1974, 73).[76] This attitude eventually reveals the human, fallible side of the heroine:

> In the end, Phèdre appears less the innocent victim than the subject of a profound moral ambivalence, bordering on the pathological. Phèdre, after all, is a sick woman, perhaps delirious in Racine as in Euripides. Lustful, jealous, self-deceiving and conscience-stricken, exhausted and bewildered by her own conflicting emotions and the twists and turns of fate, she is truly the 'weak mortal' that she claims to be. (James and Jondorf 1994, 69)

In short, the Racinian version adds a human dimension to the myth of Phaedra by presenting a cerebral and subtle passion and the heroine's own dilemmas and oscillations. In this way it departs from the rigid and larger-than-life Euripidean depiction of the heroine. Phèdre's choice of confession over concealment is, in fact, her choice of action over passivity since in

---

[76] Philip Butler (1974, 73) points out that the use of mythological characters in the tragedies of Racine is more than a mere dramatic device, used in order to raise the stature of his heroes and the excitement of the audience. Racine transforms and develops the mythological figures he chooses as heroes/heroines of his plays. "But the evocation of the myths does more than create an atmosphere, or surround the hero with the halo of legend; it is part of them, like the blood in their veins."

Racinian tragedy speech/*logos* substitutes for action/*praxis* (Barthes 1964, 58). This very choice, juxtaposed to the preference for silence in Euripides, signifies a humanization which is an aftermath of the christianized representation of the heroine's passion.

Lotan's Phaedra, however, proceeds to a consummation, thus reflecting the twentieth-century uninhibited heroine and the morally emancipated woman.

In Lotan's version, shortly after meeting Alexis and becoming aware of her feelings for him, Phaedra makes no attempt to deny it to herself or to him. The declaration of her passion for him is not a confession in the Racinian sense but an act of determination and self-affirmation. The direct admission "I am in love with you" signifies a lack of remorse and hesitation, setting apart the Euripidean and the Racinian heroines, who vacillate between μαινόμενον κακόν and ὀρθοῦσθαι γνώμην between régner and vivre, from the twentieth-century Phaedra. The notions of αἰδώς and ὀρθοῦσθαι γνώμην are personified in the novel by Anna, Phaedra's nurse and helper, who, despite her attempts to infuse Phaedra with a sense of shame and concern, in fact achieves the opposite.

Phaedra's main reaction is to succumb to her passion but this is not presented as a sign of weakness or fallibility, as in Euripides and Racine. On the contrary, it becomes a manifestation of the heroine's inner strength and determination and elevates her to the level of the tragic heroine as she defies cultural and moral norms, disregards social repercussions and shows no vacillation, no hesitation, no attempt to conceal or deny her feelings. Indeed, Lotan's version reflects the twentieth-century representation of female characters, who show more determination, and departs significantly from the passive Euripidean and Racinian heroines – in the same sense that Rita Dove's Persephone differs greatly from the Homeric hymn's or Tennyson's renditions.

Lotan's Phaedra consciously chooses to μαινόμενον κακόν disregarding all the consequences. In fact, for her, succumbing to her passion is not κακόν but ὀρθόν; in a unique amalgamation of the Classical Greek notion of fate and predestination with the modern idea of disregard for social and moral constraints Lotan justifies her heroine's passion as something natural because it was her fate to fall in love with Alexis and because the passion she experiences is powerful and profound. The heroine's reaction is a natural consequence of her own apprehension of her passion as something normal and this is a significant departure from the Classical Greek premise of passion as deviance and abnormality. Her disregard for her little son[77] is

[77] "For myself, I knew clearly and shamelessly, I would have sacrificed all for what we had, not even deeming it a sacrifice. Even if I never had another child I would

not only an indication of the powerful effect of her passion but it is also a suggestion that Ἔρως and motherhood are incompatible.

The modern Phaedra is an individualist who acts according to her own will while disregarding collective beliefs and social conventions. There are no hesitations, no regrets, no vacillations but on the contrary there is an awareness of the risk involved and of the consequences of such a peculiar relationship. There is also a remarkable pride on the part of the heroine, which is justified by the freedom of choice and will, which motivates her actions.

In all three versions, the reactions of Phaedra – silence, confession, consummation – suggest a heroine who explores different avenues of dealing with a complex situation in which she must find a harmonious resolution. Euripides presents silence as a reaction, which is a result of the Classical Greek culture of αἰδώς and εὔκλεια, while Racine prefers an exploration of the mind of his heroine through her consecutive confessions and Lotan presents a modern heroine who succumbs to passion at once.

Let us now consider the significance of death, in the form of suicide, as the only alternative to an outcome that is denied to the heroine.

In the Euripidean play the heroine's suicide constitutes a revenge on the young Hippolytus. Initially, though, her suicide was planned as an alternative and honourable solution to her embarrassing situation.[78] Although her suicide appears to be the culmination of her passion (rejected by Hippolytus and still under the effects of her "manic" state of mind she puts an end to this impossible situation by killing herself and leaves the defamatory note accusing Hippolytus of sexually assaulting her), it is, in fact, a calculated revenge on Hippolytus. Her revenge consists of her own death and a message that she leaves in which she accuses Hippolytus of making sexual advances towards her and assaulting her. Suicide can hardly be considered a form of revenge, yet for Phaedra, her own death secures the credibility of her claim against Hippolytus. When Theseus is pointing to the dead body of his wife he perceives it as a proof of his son's guilt: "This fact that does not speak proclaims your wickedness." (Euripides 1995, 113) Through the death of Phaedra, Euripides empowers his heroine and gives her an instrumental role in the plot: "he has, in practice, succeeded not simply in maintaining Phaedra's influence after her death but in actually increasing her effectiveness precisely because she is dead." (Pittas-Herschbach 1990, 150) Phaedra's death confirms the classical Athenian stratagem of female silence and confinement while the manner of her death (suicide) suggests

---

never have regretted losing my little Dimitri." (Lotan 1962, 51).

[78] See Phaedra's speech to the women of Troezin where she explains her initial plan to cope with her passion. (Euripides 1995, 163-165)

the desperation and imprisonment of the heroine whose identity is reduced to her fame and reputation (αἰδώς and εὔκλεια). Eventually, Phaedra becomes her death and ironically manages to achieve what she could not achieve while alive, namely to be heard and to obtain some form of power and influence over her environment. Consequently, her suicide is not only a revenge on Hippolytus but a revenge on the fifth-century Athenian female-disempowering culture.

In Racine, Phèdre's death is the punishment that she consciously decides to impose on herself in order to purify herself from her guilt and her incestuous passion. Her death takes place after Hippolyte's so it is clearly an attempt to cleanse her guilt of the death of the innocent Hippolyte. When earlier in the play she confesses to Hippolyte and acknowledges once more the inappropriate nature of her feelings she invites him to kill her as a punishment for her transgression.[79] She has allowed herself to become monstrous, and this monster must be killed. Butler comments that "death offers no relief: it is no longer the ultimate shelter, the compassionate night of nothingness, but the promise of the Last Judgement and eternal torment." (Butler 1974, 85)

In her final confession to Theseus, while she is dying, Phèdre admits her guilt and seeks purification and forgiveness in a christianized ending which contrasts greatly with the revengeful ending of the Euripidean play. Shaw notes that Phèdre "represents a final stage in the humanisation of the perfect baroque hero" (Shaw 1980, 58). Racine discards the Euripidean cosmic framework in favour of a homocentric Weltanschauung which is manifested in his preoccupation with the 'inner' heroes; the ending of *Phèdre* is indeed in accordance with this Racinian, and baroque Weltanschauung.

However, despite this seemingly strong contrast between the pagan, revengeful Phaedra and the christianized, repentant Phèdre both endings reveal a view of passion as something atrocious that generates evil and must be extinguished.

Lotan's Phaedra resorts to suicide as an escape and an alleviation from a great suffering. Phaedra herself refers to it as a "sleep", thus conveying her desire for peace and relief.

---

[79] Phèdre's invitation to be killed by Hippolyte by seizing his sword and pointing to her chest is also seen as a final, desperate attempt to seduce Hippolyte. I believe that this seductive feeling is mostly unconscious while the will to a cathartic death is conscious, and it is precisely this dual significance of the scene that manifests the frustration of the heroine.

> It is all over now and I want to sleep. Anna knows me so well that I don't have to speak. I have said my goodbyes and she is still here, holding death in a small bottle in her hands, forever ready to serve me. (Lotan 1962, 151)

Phaedra's resolution to 'sleep' comes right after Alexis' death, and her conviction that it is all over shows her death as a reaction to Alexis' death. She does not commit suicide as a way of cleansing herself nor as a result of guilt but because her passion has been denied to her and her lover is dead. Her death is a manifestation of her wish to escape with Alexis – "Come, my love. Let's leave this place" (ibid., 150) – to a locus where her passion would be legitimate and allowed to her. Consistent with her portrayal of passion from a non-judgemental and subjective perspective, Lotan opts for an ending that does not render passion as inappropriate or punishable but as simply not compatible with the circumstances.

In short, the portrait of Phaedra emerging from these three versions is that of a woman who is faced with an intense struggle with her passion. The preceding comparative analysis of the three versions of the myth of Phaedra has aimed at showing the impossibility of female passion through a discussion of the dynamics of Ἔρως in the three different version of the myth of Phaedra.

This notion of an unrealizable passion denied to the heroine permeates *The Great Chimera* which is a modern account of a woman's struggle not only with her own sexuality (we saw a struggle of that kind in Lorca's *Yerma*) but also with her incestuous erotic passion for her brother-in-law, Minas.[80] The very title of the novel encapsulates the idea of the unattainable, the evanescent, the elusive. Marina, the heroine, embarks on a quest for her sexual identity and fulfilment early in the novel, and she seems to achieve it when she meets her husband Yiannis. However, she develops a strong passion for her brother-in-law, Minas, which agitates her mentally and emotionally and becomes her own personal chimera. This passion is a comprehensive one: it includes cerebral, emotional and sexual appeal. Karagatsis's heroine displays fluctuating reactions to her passion including denial, shame, frustration and, in the end, consummation. Ultimately, it is due to the comprehensiveness of her passion that this remains unrealizable. Moreover, the death of her child constitutes a punishment for her, while suggesting that motherhood and sexuality are incompatible, a premise that is prevalent in Lorca's *Yerma* though illustrated in a completely different manner and discussed from a different point of view.

---

[80] The novel was first published in 1936 with the title *Chimera* but was revised and republished in 1953 with the title *The Great Chimera* (Beaton 1999, 144).

In the following pages I will attempt to challenge the traditional interpretation of the novel as a "sexual" work of Karagatsis by showing that the heroine is not a lust-driven Maenad but a woman who experiences an Ἔρως which is eventually denied to her.

The beginning of the novel contains a very important scene in which the heroine, an eminent scholar of Classical Greek literature, dreams of the mythological creature of Chimera after having seen a Greek ship named "Chimera" at the port of her hometown Rouen. The Chimera of her dream, however, differs from the mythological creature as it is a hybrid of a griffin and a Chimera, having the appearance of a griffin while being perceived within the dream as a Chimera. This bizarre winged Chimera, seated on Marina's bed, flees as soon as the heroine attempts to reach it. The dream, apart from its ominous symbolic quality, encapsulates the heroine's vain quest for Ἔρως and the elusiveness or in fact the denial of Ἔρως, clearly illustrated in her attempt to reach the winged creature and in its subsequent departure. The symbolic significance of the Chimera lies in its popular associations with the imaginary, and hence unattainable, but also in its mythological importance as the epitome of monstrosity.[81] The temporal and geographical location of the dream (Marina's parental house in Rouen after the death of her licentious mother) is also of great significance: despite Marina's initial renunciation of sex, sexuality and any form of romantic liaison, which comes as a reaction to her mother's licentious behaviour, the young woman is unconsciously in search of Ἔρως which, according to her ominous dream, she will never attain.

Karagatsis wrote this novel after the French author Roger Vercel gave him the idea of writing the story of a French woman who marries a Greek captain and the problems of maladjustment she faces once she finds herself living in a foreign country. The novel therefore sets off as a study of the cultural shock that a foreign woman experiences in Greece and it is part of the Karagatsean trilogy, "Εγκλιματισμός κάτω από τον Φοίβο"/ "Acclimatization under Phoebus" which examines the effects of the Apollonian light on the psyche of Northern heroes.[82] In the case of Marina, it is not simply the

---

[81] In Greek mythology Chimera (Χίμαιρα) was one of the children of Echidna and Typhon (the others being Cerberus, Sphinx and Hydra of Lerna) and it was a fire-sprouting monster with the head of a lion, the body of a goat and the tail of a serpent. This excessively hybridic and peculiar monstrosity eventually gave rise to the meaning of the word chimera as something unreal and hence unachievable and unattainable.

[82] The other two novels of the trilogy are *Colonel Liapkine* – the story of a colonel of the Russian army who escapes to Greece after the Communist Revolution, and *Jungerman* which is the story of a Finnish man living in Greece.

acclimatization (or rather the attempt at it) of foreign ideas as Beaton argues in his socio-historically oriented reading of the trilogy (Beaton 1999, 145), but also the use of the Hellenic context as an occasion for the emergence and exploration of unconscious and latent conflicts in the heroine.[83]

The first encounter between Marina and Minas is at her own wedding to Yiannis (Minas's brother) during which she is not only indifferent to her brother-in-law but she even finds him quite effeminate in contrast to the virile and sexually effervescent Yiannis. Marina's first impression of her brother-in-law is:

> ...ἓνας ἒφηβος ὣς εἲκοσι χρόνων, λιγνός καί λυγερός, μέ πρόσωπο ὂμορφο κι ἐξαιρετικά ἐκφραστικό. Ὃλη του ἡ ὑπόσταση ἀνάδινε κάτι ἀπό τήν κακοκρυμμένη συγκίνηση τοῦ θηλυκοῦ· κάτι τό λεπτά εὐαίσθητο, τό ρευστό κι ἂπιαστο. "Une femme manquée", εἶχε σκεφθεῖ, τότε. (Karagatsis 1992, 82)

> ...a teenager up to twenty years old, slim and slender, with a beautiful and particularly expressive face. His whole existence emanated something of the badly-hidden emotion of a female; something slightly sensitive, fluid and intangible. "Une femme manquée", she had thought at the time. (My translation)

The contrast between this "femme manquée" and the virile man that she is married to (precisely because of his sexual appeal) is a strong reminder of the contrast between the refined Hippolytus and the masculine Theseus.[84] Nonetheless, Marina's attraction towards Minas is not manifested as a coupe de foudre as this first encounter occurs during the first stages of her relationship with Yiannis when she is still under the elation of her newly-discovered sexuality that her husband's virility has managed to help her achieve: hence her initial impression of Minas as a "femme manqué".
This first impression however changes during their second encounter, when Minas comes to spend Christmas with them and he gradually impresses Marina not only with his physical traits but also with his charismatic personality.

---

[83] While Karagatsis in all the novels of this trilogy, but mostly in *The Great Chimera*, touches upon the Romantic distinctions between the rational North and the exotic, temperamental South he nonetheless transcends this binary by focusing on the universal appeal of the heroes' conflicts and emotions.

[84] Yiannis is a strong, virile seaman, a very pragmatic businessman, and the only man with whom Marina has experienced sexual satisfaction and fulfilment. His brother Minas on the other hand is a refined and delicate academic immersed in his scholarly activities.

Ἡ Μαρίνα τόν κοιτάει, τόν περιεργάζεται, λές καί τόν βλέπει γιά πρώτη φορά. Τότε, στό γάμο της, δέν τόν εἶχε πολυπροσέξει. "Εἶναι ὄμορφος", παραδέχτηκε. "Κάτι πιό πολύ: ἔχει μιάν ἀρχοντιά ουσική, πού πολύ σπάνια τή χαρίζει ὁ Πλάστης στούς ἀνθρώπους. Νά ἰδοῦμε, τί νόηση καί τί εὐαισθησία κρύβονται σ'αὐτό τό ἐξαίρετο σαρκικό περίβλημα." (ibid., 101)

Marina looks at him and observes him as if she sees him for the first time. Back then, at her wedding she hadn't really noticed him. 'He is beautiful', she admitted. 'And more than that: he has a natural grace, of the kind that is rarely granted to humans by God. Let's see what kind of intelligence and sensitivity are hidden inside this superb fleshly attire. (My translation)

This time in Marina's eyes Minas's refined and delicate nature is not seen as effeminacy but as grace and dignity. Her passion for him is still at a latent stage and manifests itself as a response to the magnetism of Minas's personal charisma. The reference to Minas's beauty and natural grace echoes Phèdre's description of Hippolyte as "enchanting, young, the darling of all hearts, fair as the gods" (Racine 1970, 175). Despite the fact that the author never confirmed that he based his novel on the myth of Phaedra, a possible influence of this story would validate the argument of the establishment of new links between myth and literary text. Nonetheless, the relationship between Phaedra and Marina is not reduced to superficial and obvious similarities but consists of the main link between the fundamental myth of Phaedra and Karagatsis's heroine: the impossibility of a comprehensive female passion.

Karagatsis presents an attraction which develops gradually and which initially manifests itself primarily as an intellectual appeal, though the physical aspect is not undermined either. In fact, it is Minas's physical attributes that capture Marina's attention and instigate her curiosity concerning his intellectual and emotional attributes, as the heroine becomes familiar with his personality and his intellectual preoccupations. During Marina's first long discussion with Minas, the two of them talk about literature on a very sophisticated level and when, upon Marina's request to speak in French, Minas responds in ancient Greek she becomes excited.

Ὁ Μηνᾶς τήν κοιτάει μέ ματιά διαπεραστική:
-Μήπως προτιμᾶς να μιλήσουμε ἀρχαῖα ἑλληνικά; Ἔμαθα πώς εἶσαι δυνατή…
Ξαναλέει ὅσα εἶπε, σέ ἄμεμτη ἀττική διάλεχτο, καί μέ προφορά ἐρασμιακή.
Ἡ Μαρίνα ἐρεθίζεται· σηκώνεται ὄρθια, τοῦ ἀπαντάει.
(Karagatsis 1992, 106)

Minas looks at her with a piercing glance:

– Would you perhaps prefer to talk in ancient Greek? I was told that you are good….
He repeats what he said, in an impeccable attic dialect and with an Erasmian intonation. Marina is stimulated; she stands up and replies to him.
(My translation)

The significance of this scene is further highlighted through the reaction of Marina's mother-in-law, Reizena, who represents traditional morality but is also a prophetic figure throughout the novel.

Ὁ Γιάννης διασκεδάζει φοβερά. Ὄχι ὅμως κι ἡ Ρεΐζαινα. Κάθεται μέ τόν κορμό ὀρθό, τα χέρια σταυρωμένα στά γόνατά της. Τά μάτια της παρακολουθοῦν κάποιαν ὁρατή γι' αὐτά σκέψη. Δέν ἦταν ἔτσι πού πρόσμενε νά χαρεῖ τόν ἐρχομό τοῦ μικροῦ της γιοῦ. Κάτι καινούργιο μπῆκε μέσα στό σπίτι· κάτι πού διαποτίζει καί μεταλλάζει ἐκείνο πού ἀπό πάντοτε ὑπῆρχε…(ibid.)

Yiannis is terribly amused. But not Reizena. She is sitting with her torso straight, her hands crossed on her knees. Her eyes seem to be following an inner thought. This was not what she had in mind while anticipating her youngest son's visit. Something new had just entered their home; something that permeates and transforms what already exists… (My translation)

Reizena, whose presence as the prophetic old woman in the novel is an echo of the Classical notions of αἰδώς and εὔκλεια senses that this immediate communication between Minas and Marina is the onset of a strong passion. She is able to foresee the ominous significance of this "something new" which penetrated her home and which is bound to transform their lives dramatically. Indeed, this scene signifies the birth of this passion, as Marina's wish to discover what is hidden "in this superb fleshly attire" is gradually realized as her attraction to Minas increases. Her strong academic background as a Classical Greek scholar enables her not only to appreciate but also to pursue this highly intellectualized communication.

This second encounter with Minas causes Marina further agitation which manifests itself in insomnia. Her attempt to overcome her insomnia with a book is unsuccessful as thoughts and reflections on her brother-in-law dominate her mind: "Τώρα μπορῶ νά πῶ πώς τόν γνωρίζω. Ὄχι, ὁ ἀρχικός μου χαρακτηρισμός – une femme manquée – δέν στέκεται." (ibid., 107) "Now I can say that I know him. No, my initial characterization – une femme manquée – is not true." (My translation)

As she is mentally processing and evaluating her encounter with Minas she finds herself developing an admiration for, and affinity with, him.

> Νοήμων, καλλιεργημένος, λεπταίσθητος. Στό ἀριστοκρατικό βιολογικά σάρκινο περίβλημα φωλιάζει ἠθικός κόσμος ἀριστοκρατικός. Δέν μπορῶ νά μή θαυμάσω τό κριτικό πνεῦμα πού συνοδεύει τήν πλατειά του καλλιέργεια. Κι εἶναι μόλις εἴκοσι χρόνων! Τό σημαντικότερο όμως σ'αὐτόν εἶναι ἡ νοοτροπία του, ἡ τόσο πρωτότυπη καί διεισδυτική, ἀλλά καί ὀρθολογικά πειθαρχημένη κάτω ἀπ'τόν ἁρμονικό συνταυτισμό τῆς γνώσης μέ τό συναίσθημα.(ibid., 108)
>
> Intelligent, cultivated, refined. Inside his noble fleshly cloak lies a noble mental realm. I cannot but admire his critical spirit which complements his broad education. And he is only twenty years old! But the most important thing about him is his mentality, so original and incisive but also rationally disciplined under the harmonious symbiosis of knowledge and emotion. (My translation)

Marina's attraction consists of a combination of physical (ἀριστοκρατικό βιολογικά σάρκινο περίβλημα), mental and emotional (ἁρμονικό συνταυτισμό τῆς γνώσης μέ τό συναίσθημα) appeal.

The powerful influence of Minas over Marina, not only on an intellectual but also on a sexual level, is further manifested in her inability to respond to her husband's sexual advances that same night: "Ἔνιωσε τό θερμό χέρι του ν'ἀναζητάει τό κορμί της. Τρεμούλιασε καί σφάλησε τά μάτια…" (ibid., 109*)* (She felt his warm hand searching for her body. She trembled and closed her eyes) (My translation). Her rejection of sexual intercourse is an indicator of the sexual nuances that underlie her attraction to Minas. Not only does she find him graceful and beautiful, but she is also excited by his intellectual qualities and, this kind of dual attraction towards him (physical and mental) has such a profound impact on her that she feels her own husband's attempt to approach her sexually as a violation not only of her body but also of the whole mental experience she is enjoying while thinking of Minas.

The rapport between the two develops further when Marina visits Athens for the first time and Minas is her host and guide; the intellectual allure develops into a different kind of kinship when a subtle yet clear flirtation between them begins to develop. Marina engages in witty, flirtatious comments when she is with him. She admires his profound and extensive knowledge of archaeology and art while they are in the Acropolis and the Archaeological Museum, and he explains to her the historical and artistic qualities of each work. The culmination of their visit to the antiquities is when Minas introduces her to "the woman I love" (ibid., 156 My translation), who in fact is the statue of a Kore. Marina sees in his attraction to this statue a cerebral passion, the amalgamation of the aesthetic with the intellectual and this constitutes an epiphany for her:

> Σήκωσε πάλι τά μάτια καί κοίταξε τήν πέτρινη γυναίκα μέ τήν ἀλαζονική μορφή καί τά εἰρωνικά, τά λεπταίσθητα ἡδονόφιλα χείλια. Κι ἔξαφνα, ὡσάν κάτι ἀπροσδόκητο νά τῆς ἀποκαλύφθηκε, ἔνιωθε νά τήν κυριεύει δυσφορία ἀσφυκτική. (ibid.,157)

> She lifted her eyes again and looked at the marble woman with the arrogant face and the ironic, finely hedonistic lips. And suddenly, she felt overwhelmed by a suffocating discomfort, as if something unexpected had just been revealed to her. (My translation)

The enigmatic figure of the Kore agitates her and constitutes a premonition of the conclusion of this passion. The proud statue with its refined, plain beauty, its geometrical aestheticism and its ironic hedonism suddenly communicates to her, her own experience of an amalgamation of the physical and the intellectual. Her discomfort and temporary sickness that day in the Museum is mostly a result of her realization of her passion for Minas. More particularly the realization of the inappropriate nature of her feelings inflicts a physical sickness on her similar to the sickness that Phaedra experiences upon realization of her powerful passion for Hippolytus. The statue of the Kore reminds her that mind and body are complementary and that profound passion, which consists of sexual desire and spiritual affinity, can indeed exist.

This fusion of the intellectual and the sexual is very well illustrated in the incident of a shared poetic experience during which Marina is overwhelmed by a sensual and mental agitation complementing her experience at the Museum. While Minas is reciting a poem about Athens and they both sit on the balcony overlooking the Attic plane, she is overwhelmed by a "vibrating mental sensuality" (ibid., 160). The poem contains repeated references to nudity, nakedness, lack of inhibition and restraint, sensuality and (pro)creative urges.

> Ὅλα γυμνά τριγύρω μας,
> ὅλα γυμνά ἐδῶ πέρα,
> κάμποι, βουνά, ἀκροούρανα,
> ἀκράταγ' εἶναι ἡ μέρα.
> Διάφαν' ἡ πλάση, ὁλάνοιχτα
> τά ὁλόβαθα παλάτια·
> τό φῶς χορτάστε, μάτια,
> κιθάρες, τό ρυθμό. (ibid., 159)

> Everything bare all around,/ everything bare right here,/ fields, mountains, the edge of sky,/ the day pours in and near./ All of creation crystal clear,/ the palaces wide open;/ eyes feed upon the endless light,/ and lyres upon the rhythm. (My translation)

The beginning of the recital clearly suggests physical as well as emotional and mental nakedness, and the formidable power of illumination, truth in its physical, metaphorical and cosmogonic sense. Marina's subsequent attempt to stop Minas's recitation, by suggesting that it is time for dinner, reveals her wish to shun such a perilous and painful terrain, choosing instead oblivion, concealment, a state of μη γιγνώσκουσα.

The blatantly erotic imagery of the lines that follow and the underlying fusion of the sexual and the intellectual, the physical and the metaphysical, the mundane and the conceptual, remind her of the Kore statue in the Museum and the overwhelming effect it had on her. References to "Ἐδῶ τά πάντα ξέστηθα/κι ἀδιάντροπα λυσσᾶνε" – "everything here bare-chested and shamelessly raving", to the flesh which is "fire" ("καί τό κορμί φωτιά'ναι") and to the "ὀλύμπιο τό νεχτάρι/τῆς γύμνιας" – "the olympian nectar of bareness" highlight the theme of sexuality and sublimation. "Ἀνατρίχιασε. Θά ἤθελε νά τοῦ πεῖ νά πάψει, νά σταματήσει. Μά δέν βρῆκε δύναμη." (ibid., 160) – "She shivered. She wanted to ask him to stop; but she didn't find the strength." (My translation)

As Minas continues his reciting, Karagatsis, through the verses of Kostis Palamas, articulates the crux of the passion of his heroine: "Καί παῖξε καί παράστησε/τά ἡδονικά, τά ὡραῖα,/λαγάρισε τή γύμνια σου/καί κάμε την ἰδέα" (ibid., 161) – and so enact and show/the beautiful and the pleasurable/filter your bareness and transform it to an idea (My translation.)

The transformation of the bare flesh into an idea typifies the pivotal notion of the novel which is the comprehensive female passion in which the sexual, the emotional and the intellectual are fused and constitute merely different facets of the same experience.

> Ἄνοιξε τά μάτια καί κοίταξε τό Μηνᾶ, πού εἶχε παρατήσει τό βιβλίο κι ἀπάγγελνε ἀπ'ἔξω, ἔχοντας τά μάτια του ἀφημένα πέρα, στόν ἀκαθόριστο καί φωτεινό ὁρίζοντα τῆς θάλασσας. Κι ἦταν τά μάτια του ὀρθάνοιχτα κι ὁλοκάθαρα· κι ἦταν ἡ μορφή του ἐξαγνισμένη ἀπό κάθε ἀντικαθρέφτισμα ἐνστίκτου. Δάγκωσε τά χείλια καί ξανάκλεισε τά μάτια. (ibid., 161)
>
> She opened her eyes and looked at Minas, who had left the book and was reciting by heart, his eyes looking afar at the indefinite and light horizon of the sea. And his eyes were wide open and crystal clear; and his face was purified from any reflection of instinct. She bit her lips and closed her eyes again. (My translation)

This scene comes as a natural consequence of the scene in the Museum in front of the statue of the Kore. While Minas is reciting the poem Marina begins to experience this combination of mental and aesthetic exhilaration which emanates from the powerful text of the poem and the beauty of its language, enhanced by the refined, beautiful features of the person who is reciting it.

After her return from the Acropolis and the "vibrating mental sensuality" that she experiences when Minas recites a poem to her, she feels guilty for her thoughts and admits to herself, "What a disgustingly corrupt person I am!" (ibid., 164)

After the first epiphany in the Museum, Marina now experiences a second illumination, or rather realization. She feels guilty for the first time for the way she responds to her brother-in-law and for this "different" excitement she experiences every time she is with him. The feelings of guilt and the admission of the inappropriate nature of her attraction to her brother-in-law constitute Marina's own acknowledgement of her passion.

Her return to Syros, which is an opportunity for her to recollect her days in Athens and assess anew the entire experience in the safe environment of her marriage, reveals the strong impact that Minas has on her as his image invades every memory and instigates Marina's desire to discover more about him.

> Ἡ μορφή τοῦ Μηνᾶ συμπλήρωνε τήν κάθε εἰκόνα. Ἤρεμη τώρα, μέσα στήν μέ προσπάθεια κερδισμένη ὀργανική της ἰσορροπία, προσπαθοῦσε νά ἀξιολογήσει τό μικρό κουνιάδο. Ὁ εκλεπτισμός, ὁ ἀπαραμείωτος συναισθηματισμός, ἡ ἄκρα εὐαισθησία, ὁ αὐθορμητισμός τῶν σπάνιων ψυχικῶν ἐκδηλώσεων, ἡ διεισδυτική νοημοσύνη, πού ἒφτανε ὣς τήν ἀποκρυφότερη ψυχική πτυχή τοῦ διπλανοῦ του, τοῦ δημιουργοῦσαν προσωπικότητα ξεχωριστοῦ και γοητευτικοῦ ἄντρα....
>
> ....Ὁπωσδήποτε ἦταν ἄντρας ἑλκυστικός μέσα στόν ψυχρό σκεπτικισμό του·... (ibid., 169-170)

> Minas' image completed every picture. Peaceful and in a balance achieved after effort, she attempted to assess her young brother-in-law. His refined and intense sentimentality, his sharp sensitivity, his impulsive expression of his rare emotions, his incisive intelligence which reached the innermost psychic regions of others gave him the personality of a special and charming man.
>
> He was definitely an attractive man within his cold scepticism.
>
> (My translation)

Marina attempts to rationalize her situation and thus convince herself that she cannot possibly feel attracted to another man by reminding herself that Yiannis still exercises a great influence on her since he is the first man who gave her sexual pleasure. His virility and his straightforward manly attitude enslave her body and heart. Subconsciously, Marina tries to rationalize and intellectualize the situation and convince herself of the significance of her husband in her life. She actually tries to convince herself that since Yiannis was the only man with whom she experienced sexual satisfaction she can only be attracted to him. At this stage Marina is still in denial regarding her passion for Minas and like the Euripidean Phaedra she chooses to be μη γιγνώσκουσα.

The strong contrast between Yiannis and Minas, and the effect it has on Marina, is strongly reminiscent of the difference between Theseus and Hippolytus in the myth of Phaedra. While Yiannis and Theseus represent masculinity in its traditional and more physical sense, Minas and Hippolytus stand for the more intellectual and refined aspects of manliness. In both cases, the heroine is desperately attracted to the latter version of masculinity which elicits profound and powerful emotions in her. In Euripides's play the heroine is also attracted to Hippolytus's refined appearance which is matched by his spirituality and virtue. His preoccupation with hunting is not an exercise of his masculinity but on the contrary falls within the pious worship of Artemis. His refined nature therefore contrasts greatly with the rough, almost barbaric nature of his father, Theseus, who is renowned for his encounters with monsters, his extraordinary adventures in distant lands and last but not least his lustful and promiscuous temperament. On the other hand, Yiannis is a loyal and monogamous partner, yet he is a pragmatic man who cannot perceive the subtleties of life and cannot communicate with his wife on a mental level. His preoccupation with shipping and the sea contrasts greatly with Minas's scholarly and intellectual concerns in the same manner that Theseus's adventurous spirit contrasts with Hippolytus's refined nature.

Marina's mental experiment is taken a bit further as she is determined to prove to herself that her sexuality is so strongly attached to Yiannis that even the mere thought of intercourse with another man will elicit reactions of disgust and detestation in her.

> Ὄχι, κανείς ἐξόν ἀπ'τό δικό της ἄντρα δέν μπόρεσε νά τῆς γεννήσει τόν παραμικρό πειρασμό. Ἐπίμονη στούς αὐτοπειραματισμούς, προσπάθησε νά κάνει κάτι ἄλλο: ὅταν ὁ Γιάννης τήν ἀγκάλιαζε, προσπαθοῦσε νά φαντασθεῖ πώς στή θέση του ἦταν κάποιος ἀπό τούς τόσους ἄντρες πού γνώριζε, ἤ πού μονάχα εἶχε ἰδεῖ. Μόλις ὅμως ὁ φανταστικός "ἄλλος" ὑποκαθιστοῦσε τήν πραγματικότητα τοῦ Γιάννη, ἀμέσως ἡ παλιά ἀπέχθεια πρός τό σερνικό ξυπνοῦσε καί τῆς ἔκοβε τήν ὁρμή, σάν μέ μαχαίρι. Μέ κίνηση ἀσυναίσθητη, ἀντανακλαστική, τέντωνε τά χέρια νά διώξει ἀπό πάνω της τό σιχαμερό κορμί. Μά τά χέρια της ἔρχονταν σ'ἐπαφή μέ τήν ὑλική πραγματικότητα τοῦ Γιάννη· καί ξαναβυθιζόταν στό χάος τῆς γλύκας… (ibid., 138-139)

No, no man except her husband could cause the slightest temptation to her. Being persistent in experimentations, she tried to do something else: every

> time Yiannis embraced her, she would try to imagine somebody else in his place, some one of the men she knew or had just seen. Yet, when this imaginary "other man" would substitute Yiannis's reality, immediately the old repulsion towards the male would awaken and cut her impulse like a knife. With an unconscious, reflexive movement, she would stretch her hands in order to push away the disgusting body. But her hands would touch the material reality of Yiannis and then she would again be immersed into a chaos of delight. (My translation)

This peculiar experiment reveals Marina's frustration in her vain attempt to rationalize every single experience and emotion. The fantasy that Marina creates, highly reminiscent of Phèdre's hallucinatory *aveu*, offers an insight into her mental condition and manifests her wish to be ignorant and remain in denial.

Soon, however, Marina discovers that there is another male who does not elicit feelings of repulsion and disgust but on the contrary instigates a profound longing and desire in her. This man is Minas, her brother-in-law.

> Μιά νύχτα ὃμως, στερνός στήν ἀλληλουχία τῶν ἀποτυχημένων ἐραστῶν τῆς φαντασίας της, ἦρθε καί κάποιος πού – ὁπωσδήποτε – δέν ἒπρεπε νά ἒρθει. Ἦρθε μονάχος του, χωρίς ἡ δική της θέληση νά τόν προσκαλέσει. Κι αὐτός δέν γέννησε τήν ἀπέχθεια τῶν ἄλλων. Γι'αὐτόν, ἡ Μαρίνα ἂπλωσε τά χέρια ὂχι ὃπως γιά τούς ἄλλους, μά μέ λαχτάρα νά ἀγκαλιάσει τό περιπόθητο κι ἀνύπαρκτο κορμί. Κι ὃταν τά χέρια της συναπάντησαν τή γνωστή σάρκα, ὁ σπασμός πού εἶχε ἀρχίσει νά συνταράζει τά σωθικά της ἒσπασε ἀπότομα, κομμένος ἀπό μαχαιριά ὀδυνηρή…(ibid., 139)

> But one night, last in the sequence of her failed imaginary lovers, there came another one who, certainly, should have come. And this one didn't create the repulsion that the others did. For him, Marina stretched her hands not as she did for the others, but with longing to touch the much desired and non-existing body. And when her hands met the familiar flesh, the spasm that had started shaking inside her, stopped immediately, cut by a painful knife. (My translation)

This scene of the metamorphosis of the husband into the desired lover is similar to the scene described in Phèdre's soliloquy in Racine where she fantasizes about Hippolyte as a metamorphosized Theseus. This hybrid, imaginary lover manifests Marina's confusion and emotional chaos. This metamorphosis can be seen as an attempt to legitimize the inappropriate desire for a man other than the husband. This confusion between the inappropriate desire for this other man and the acceptance of the husband, also manifested in Yerma's frustration over Victor and Juan, illustrates the great impasse of the heroines and their entrapment in a predicament that denies them the right to be celebrants of Ἔρως.

In a striking similarity to Phaedra, Marina carries the inheritance of this peculiar binary in her character: reason and restraint inherited from her father, and passion and lust from her mother. Her father is an army General with an austere appearance and a reserved, self-disciplined character, representing order, constraint and normality: "He would always arrive without any notice. He'd look at mother with his grey cold eyes, kiss his daughter and then he would be silent. He would be silent for fifteen consecutive days." (ibid., 25) His wife, on the other hand, is an impulsive and promiscuous woman who has always been "liberated from prejudices and moral inhibitions" (ibid., 29-30) and who after her husband's death turns her house into an unofficial brothel. This antithetical parental bequest echoes the contrariness in Phaedra's dual inheritance: reason and restraint from her father Minos, the judge, and uninhibited sexuality and transgression from her mother Pasiphae, the adulteress and transgressor of sexual boundaries. In that sense Marina is indeed very similar to Phaedra: bound to vacillate between reason and passion, between order and chaos, between restraint and licentiousness, between *régner* and *vivre*.

Marina is a very intelligent woman who intellectualizes every experience and lives life on a highly cerebral level. Consequently, her struggle with her passion for Minas takes place on a mental plane where she tries to rationalize her feelings as a way of fighting her passion. Her own full realization of her true feelings for Minas comes towards the end of the novel after she has exhausted all her rational arguments and justification, and she is left with virtually no other choice than to face her passion.

After the dream in which Minas takes the place of Yiannis, Marina experiences a sense of physical and emotional frailty. The following morning, she wakes up feeling sick, her limbs feeling weak and her soul feeling depressed. Marina's rationality, though, dictates to her that she should suppress the feelings for Minas and continue her life regardless: "Indeed after an hour she was again healthy, cheerful and balanced; simply because her reason dictated to her that this is how it should be." (ibid., 140)

The final encounter between Minas and Marina is when little Anna, her daughter, is seriously ill and the two meet in a tense atmosphere. In that scene passion prevails, and the two end up copulating bestially while little Anna is dying in the next room.

> Ἀπόμειναν ἀντιμέτωποι, ἀμίλητοι. Τά μάτια της γυάλιζαν σάν πράσινα ἀστέρια· ἡ ἀνάσα της ἦταν κοντή κι ἄρρυθμη. Ἐκεῖνος ἔνιωσε τή ναρκωμένη δύναμή του νά ξυπνάει, νά τόν πλημμυράει, νά τόν κάνει πρωτόγονο σερνικό, ὥς τό στερνό του κύτταρο. Πράσιν'ἀστέρια γίνηκαν

> καί τά δικά του μάτια. Ἀνοιγόκλεισε τά δάχτυλα, σάν τόν τίγρη πού δοκιμάζει τά νύχια του πρίν ἐπιτεθεῖ. Τά χείλια του μισόπαιζαν καί φάνηκαν τά τιγρίσια δόντια του, ἄσπρα κι ἀπειλητικά. Ἡ γυναίκα στυλώθηκε, ἕτοιμη ν'ἀντιμετωπίσει τό θανατερό ἀγώνα πού γύρευε, πού προκαλοῦσε. Μέσα στ'ἀδύναμο πορτοκαλί ἀντιφέγγισμα, τά δυό θεριά ἀναμετρήθηκαν ἀπ΄τήν κορφή ὥς τά νύχια. Τά ρουθούνια τους ἔπαιξαν μέ παλμό σπασμωδικό, ἀνάσαιναν τίς ὀσμές ὁ ἕνας τ'ἀλλουνοῦ. Ἦσαν ἕτοιμοι. (ibid., 371-372)

> They stayed there facing each other speechless. Her eyes were shining like two green stars; her breath was short and with no pace. He felt his dormant power awakening, overwhelming him, making him a primitive male to the last cell. His eyes too became green stars. He opened and closed his fingers like a tiger before attacking. His lips were trembling revealing his tiger teeth, white and threatening. The woman stood up, ready to face the fatal fight that she was asking for, that she was provoking. In the faint orange evening light the two beasts encountered from top to toe. Their nostrils moved spasmodically, they were breathing each other's odours. They were ready. (My translation)

There is a dual significance to this highly charged scene which illustrates the culmination of Marina's passion. The diction and imagery, borrowed from the animal kingdom, suggest, on the one hand, the completion of an intellectual and cerebral passion with the procreative urge. The description of the encounter, on the other hand, creates the atmosphere of a fight between two ferocious animals: the "primitive male" who opens and closes his fingers "like a tiger before attacking" "revealing his tiger teeth" and the trembling of the nostrils, are powerful images that render the high tension and the animalistic nature of the encounter. The scene of the sexual encounter between Marina and Minas, juxtaposed with their previous intellectual and emotional encounters, creates the comprehensive view of female passion as a sexual, emotional, and cerebral experience, and emphasizes the eventual denial of this passion to the heroine. The timing of the encounter, while Marina's daughter is ill and dying, further accentuates the denial: while Marina consummates and completes her passion she is deprived of motherhood as a preamble to her deprivation of passion itself. The death of her daughter serves as a punishment for the consummation of her passion and later on the death of Minas highlights the impossibility of this passion.

Even today Karagatsis is often referred to as a writer obsessed with sexuality in its sheer animalistic, carnal form while a careful and critical investigation of his texts proves exactly the opposite: Karagatsis acknowledged the significance of sexuality while searching for its fusion with the mind. While sex is presented as a physical urge in his works his heroes are also in search of the ultimate experience of a sexual, emotional and mental connection, in other words of Ἔρως. *The Great Chimera* is a magnificent illustration of his own conviction that this unique fusion is possible. Contrary to the critical belief that "In *Chimera* Karagatsis separates man-intellect from man-flesh" (Kokkinaki 1991, 58), the novel itself proves that he was actually arguing for an amalgamation of the two, which constitutes a true passion.

Thanassis Tzoulis in his essay "Need and desire in the work of M. Karagatsis" argues that despite the critical consensus which has labelled Karagatsis a Freudian writer and a second-class naturalist, a careful study of his work reveals exactly the opposite: in Karagatsis's novels there is indeed a satisfaction of sexual impulse and sexual need but there is no satisfaction of the profound erotic desire. Tzoulis draws a distinction between *need* and *desire*, the former being the mere physical sexual urge and the latter being the profound erotic desire which is a fusion of pure physicality and emotional, mental correspondence, and originates in an unconscious demand (*demande*) for integration and fulfilment (Tzoulis 1993, 185-224). This inner demand is the necessity for Ἔρως. Indeed, Karagatsis's heroes are actually in quest of the satisfaction of this inner desire but they only manage to achieve the satisfaction of their very basic and profane urges. In the case of Marina, her need is fulfilled by her husband, yet her desire is still unfulfilled and unrealized, and her passion for Minas is the manifestation of the search for the fulfilment of this desire.

The fundamental myth of Phaedra, distilled in this chapter, pertains precisely to this inner desire which transcends the sexual and the emotional, and constitutes an almost existential quest. The essential element in the myth of Phaedra which applies to Marina is the metaphysical apprehension of Ἔρως. The constant search of Karagatsean heroes for the fulfilment of this desire becomes an existential quest for Ἔρως which, in *The Great Chimera*, is typified in the very title of the novel. The great chimera epitomizes the elusiveness not only of Ἔρως but of existential contentment.

The denial of such a comprehensive passion is manifested first and foremost in the death of Marina's daughter which functions as a form of punishment for the admission and consummation of her passion with Minas. When Marina finally communicates her passion to Minas (in a subtle confession of her love for him) and they engage in copulation instead of monitoring little Anna's fight with fever, the little girl dies, helpless, in the next room. This incident suggests an incongruity between motherhood and the fulfilment of a comprehensive passion. In Lorca's *Yerma* we saw a lack of both passion and motherhood, while here we have a more tragic and cruel denial of both for the heroine. While Yerma cannot achieve sexual, erotic fulfilment or motherhood, Marina achieves sexual satisfaction and motherhood but as soon as she experiences a complete sexual, intellectual, erotic passion she is denied motherhood.[85] In Yerma's case it is eros in its basic, sexual sense that is denied to her, whereas in the case of Marina it is Ἔρως in its more complete and philosophical sense that becomes a forbidden experience. Both heroines display, each in her own way, the struggle and agony of sexuality, of passion, of Ἔρως.

[85] Her subsequent pregnancy, a result of her copulation with Minas, becomes eventually another denial of motherhood; as this child is considered a miasma it must be either killed or born elsewhere.

CHAPTER FOUR

ABIDING GODDESS: FEMALE LIMINALITY AND POETIC ARTICULATION IN IDWAR AL-KHARRAT'S ALEXANDRIAN NOVELS AND ROBERT GRAVES

> "This they know well: the Goddess yet abides"
> Robert Graves, 'In Her Praise'
> (Graves 1975, 238)

Idwar al-Kharrat's Alexandrian novels, *City of Saffron* and its sequel *Girls of Alexandria*, have been hailed by critics and scholars as paradigms of Egyptian modernist narrative and are often discussed in lieu of Proustian thematics of time and memory and Joycean narratological modus operandi. They have been described as a "compelling study of the powers and limitations of memory" (Amireh 1994, 62) and as "an exercise in memory, nostalgia and autobiography." (Irwin 1989, 106)

This Chapter offers a new reading of al-Kharrat's two novels, departing from the customary contextual and intertextual discussions that involve Arabic literature and European modernism. Within a par excellence comparative framework, whereby ostensible textual connections are transcended and new profound kinships are established, the two novels are discussed in the light of Robert Graves's poetic theory on creative articulation and female inspiration, as this is illustrated in various writings, lectures and works by him, and in the book *The White Goddess*.

The Chapter delineates the portrait of the White Goddess as a purely Gravesian conception and literary discourse by composing a mosaic out of Graves's various books, essays, interviews and lectures, and hence it attempts to present the White Goddess as a unified whole. Ultimately, it aspires to show how the liminality of the White Goddess, the poet's quest for her and the effect of those on poetic creativity, reveal the inextricable link between female liminality and poetic articulation in al-Kharrat's two novels exposing the catalytic role that the female liminal quality has for poetic inspiration and creativity via the dialectical relationship between the two.

As a conception the White Goddess is multi-faceted: a poetic persona (the Muse), a mythological persona (associated occasionally with deities and mythic figures), an instrument of poetic education (as Graves himself envisioned it)[86] and hence a poetic theory based on an idiosyncratic approach to inspiration, creativity, poetic consciousness and literary articulation. Primarily, it is a distilled experience of the poet himself and the "testament of a practising poet." (Seymour-Smith 1982, 400) The poem "In Dedication", a preamble to *The White Goddess* and "a manifesto for the Muse-tradition Graves championed" (Rooksby 1984, 54), renders the poet's experience of the Goddess and mostly of her liminal nature as well as his own quest for her and the implications of those on poetic articulation.

In Dedication

All saints revile her, and all sober men
Ruled by the God Apollo's golden mean—
In scorn of which I sailed to find her
In distant regions likeliest to hold her
Whom I desired above all things to know,
Sister of the mirage and echo.

It was a virtue not to stay,
To go my headstrong and heroic way
Seeking her out at the volcano's head,
Among pack ice, or where the track had faded
Beyond the cavern of the seven sleepers:
Whose broad high brow was white as any leper's.
Whose eyes were blue, with rowan-berry lips,
With hair curled honey-coloured to white hips.

The sap of Spring in the young wood a-stir
Will celebrate with green the Mother,
And every song-bird shout awhile for her;

[86] According to Graves, *The White Goddess* was also intended to be a guide to future poets.

> In a letter to me Graves terms it 'a book for poets; and was not therefore given footnotes'.... it records Graves' life-long encounter with the mystery of poetic inspiration, with the ancient riddle, 'whence the great line of poetry, the incandescent image which seem to derive from outside the poet?' (Steiner 1960, 356)

But I am gifted, even in November
Rawest of seasons, with no huge a sense
Of her nakedly worn magnificence
I forget cruelty and past betrayal,
Careless of where the next bright bolt may fall.

(Graves 1948, 5)

The first lines of the poem, introduce the Gravesian contraposition to the classical idea of poetry as an Apollonian activity, namely "a form of rhetoric, which meets society's demand for the god of rational enlightenment rather than for the impractical Muse." (Graves 1967, 97) Graves instead proposes a creativity that transcends prevalent poetic modes, literary trends, ideological demarcations and aesthetic practices; "A poet is a person who lives and thinks in a certain way. A poet doesn't necessarily write poems. It is simply an attitude, and there are a great many more poets around than meet the eye." ('Where the crakeberries grow – Robert Graves gives an account of himself to Leslie Norris', *Listener*, 28 May 1970 http://www.lib.buy.edu/~english/wwwI/influence/graves.html (accessed 3 March, 2014)

This contraposition between Apollonian and Muse poetry is typified in Graves's distinction between poets and gleemen, suggesting that true poetry transcends versification and consists of a mystical partaking of the "Theme", the mystery of life, death and the cycle of life. For Graves poetry is a way of thinking and existing. The true Gravesian poet, drawing upon the ideal poet as delineated in the Welsh *Red Book of Hergest*, is skilled in verse but also susceptible to the intoxicating power of creativity: "The art of the poet is the result of long experience and attention to the meanings of words, a carefully developed craftsmanship, and an intuitive openness to what Graves calls the poetic trance." (Snipes 1979, 13) Patrick Keane describes Graves as "a poet of ecstasy and unreason and a commonsensical rationalist who dreads excess and whose versecraft is always meticulous." (Keane 1980, 6) And while craftsmanship can be cultivated, the power of creativity is found in the experience of the White Goddess or the Muse, that is to say, in the poet's private and personal experience of the Goddess.[87]

Poetry is a particular outlook on life and a constant search for truth and knowledge. It is a profound and esoteric experience penetrating catalytically every aspect of a person's life and Robert Graves practised this belief and took his role as a poet very seriously (O'Prey 2001, 43). His ideas about poetry are not abstract arguments but they reflect a lifestyle and a poetic activity permeated by that particular way of thinking and existing.

[87] Graves (1965, 85-98) provides a thorough discussion of how poetic inspiration and linguistic skills work together during the poetic process.

The true Gravesian poet is first and foremost a celebrant of the White Goddess and more particularly of her most essential quality: her liminality.[88] The poet's personal quest for the Goddess is, in fact, the experience of her liminal nature which in turn determines this very quest and his poetic activity. Being the "sister of the mirage and echo" she cannot be discerned and comprehended by finite human perception; she is illusory and distant both for the human eye and ear: "The Goddess is akin to mirage and echo because of her elusiveness and intangibility." (Rooksby 1984, 55) She possesses the qualities of impalpability and delusion which in turn suggests that she is perhaps imaginary and chimerical. The "distant regions", which highlight the difficulty of the quest and her inaccessibility, suggest an inner remoteness: "The 'distant regions' are primarily psychic, not geographic." (Rooksby 1984, 55) She is a terra incognita located "at the volcano's head / Among pack ice, or where the track has faded / Beyond the cavern of the seven sleepers." (Graves 1948, 5) "The end of the track, the seven sleepers, the pursuit beyond the cave, all introduce a fitting element of mystery." (Rooksby 1984, 55-56) In addition, there is an emphasis on the difficulty of the poet's search in those mysterious and remote psychic locations. "The new lines extend and particularize the quest motif, the difficulties of the search being evoked by the locations. The molten heat of 'the volcano's head' contrasts with the immobile cold of 'pack ice'; physical extremes symbolizing the hardships the Goddess's devotees must be prepared to endure." (ibid., 55) In short, the poem conveys the uncertainty and opacity of the White Goddess affirming liminality as a fundamental aspect of hers while exemplifying the complexity of the poetic quest.

The mythological background behind the White Goddess, as well as the religious connotation of the very term goddess, have given rise to an apprehension of her as a real deity. Graves however "is not a believer in a supernatural deity or a life after death, and he disclaims any intention of setting up the White Goddess for universal worship." (Kirkham 1969, 198) The qualification white stands for the lunar and creative element while the term goddess epitomizes the metaphysical and inexplicable inherent in poetic activity:

> My task in writing *The White Goddess* was to provide a grammar of poetic myth for poets, not to plan witches' Sabbaths, compose litanies and design vestments for a new orgiastic sect, nor yet to preach matriarchy over a radio network. (Graves 1997, 855)

---

[88] See Palaska 2014, 154-160.

The belief in these inexplicable experiences simulates religious faith: "The Goddess may be a metaphor or may not; he cannot tell, because he has no other explanation to offer for the experiences to which he gives her name than that she causes them." (Kirkham 1969, 198)

The recurrent references to the White Goddess as the Muse, thus identifying her with the classical icon of poetic inspiration, have led many critics to identify her with the traditional Muse or even specific women that have influenced Graves's life and work, such as Laura Riding. Yet, "The Muse is a deity, but she is also a woman." (Graves 1948, 442) Undoubtedly, the Goddess can be associated occasionally with a particular woman but primarily and fundamentally she remains unidentified and undefined.

> He [Graves] was seeking a name for the abstract concept which he felt lay behind all poetic inspiration, and he found the White Goddess, in all her awesome ferocity. Whether or not Graves believes in her as a true Goddess is irrelevant: what is important for us to realize from *The White Goddess* is that, for Graves, no poet is a true poet until he devotes himself utterly to the expression of his love for her. (Day 1963, 166)

The White Goddess does not actually correspond to a mythical or fictitious deity (though Graves uses mythical references when discussing her): it actually corresponds to this "abstract concept" that lies behind poetic creativity. Graves himself has argued that "From this obsessive love of an unknown Muse proceed poems of trance, in which the ancient mythical elements assemble thickly. The Muse, I have said, is 'the perpetual other woman', never the poet's wife." (Graves 1962, 64)

By Graves's admission, the Muse is not a particular woman: she is "unknown" and is "the perpetual other woman". The word "perpetual" indicates the continuous and infinite search of the poet for her. This search, which is a manifestation of the desire for truth and knowledge, and which characterizes and distinguishes the poet, is the pursuit of knowledge, of knowing the unknown, obtaining the unobtainable. Patrick Keane (1980, 54) considers this desire for knowledge a "will to truth" which he argues is the unifying principle in the discourse of the White Goddess. The association of knowledge with the White Goddess, "whom I desired above all things to know", constitutes a sine qua non in the Gravesian poetic theory; "There is in Graves an abiding impulse to reveal the essential." (Keane 1980, 54) Indeed, the association of the liminality of the Goddess with the concept of knowledge, in conjunction with the poetic quest, signifies the very essence of the White Goddess. This will to knowledge also permeates Graves's poetic oeuvre; "The poetry of Robert Graves in a very significant sense reflects the poet's lifelong search for the meaning of existence." (Sanders 1970, 23)

Kirkham notes that "There is even a bold emphasis laid on the paradox of wanting knowledge of what may be a mirage." (Kirkham 1969, 206) In other words there, is a desire for a chimeric knowledge.

The liminality of the White Goddess is the liminality of truth and knowledge. The Muse is not merely some other woman but the "perpetual other woman", a constant reinvention of the poet which instigates and invigorates his creativity: she is the touchstone for poetic authenticity and talent. Consequently, she is never fixed but remains evanescent and intangible. Tangibility is incompatible with the "sister of the mirage and echo", with her very nature and essence. There is no comprehensive definition of her but Graves provides certain qualities of hers as they are manifested in his personal poetic experience. The very notion of liminality suggests a lack of a clear definition or rather the defiance of definition, perhaps even a transcendence of all definitions. The *White Goddess* declares that "A poet cannot continue to be a poet if he feels that he has made a permanent conquest of the Muse, that she is always his for the asking." (Graves 1948, 442) It is therefore in the very nature of the Goddess to be intangible, unattainable and evanescent, though immanent. She defies possession, locality and definition. Her existence can only be affirmed through poetic articulation, yet it may also depend on poetic consciousness. Whether she exists or not is completely irrelevant, what is important are the processes in the poetic mind while in pursuit of her, and the result of this pursuit. The "distant regions likeliest to hold her" are the deepest and most latent layers of poetic consciousness, and this paradox of an immanent yet distant White Goddess constitutes the Gravesian poetic activity. What is actually suggested here is the ultimate poetic challenge which consists of the inner, continuous and persistent pursuit of the unattainable. Neil Powell (1997, 89) points out that "Graves gave The White Goddess the subtitle, 'A Historical Grammar of Poetic Myth', though he might almost have borrowed Wordsworth's 'The Growth of a Poet's Mind.' As a matter of fact, Graves's writings on the White Goddess "tell us more about him than about the numinous Goddess." (Keane 1980, 54) In other words, the quest for the Goddess is not a quest for an "other" that exists outside the poet's mind but a quest for the poetic self, and therefore it is an inner self-quest where the poet has to delve into the "back of the mind" (Graves 1962, 10) and transcend reason.

The Goddess is a property and a product of the poetic mind, and is as immanent and intangible as poetic thought and inspiration are. For Graves "writing a poem is rather like finding the top of a statue buried in sand. You

gradually take the sand away and you find the thing, whole – That is what poetry is, rather than building something up. It's rediscovering what you've known inside yourself the whole time, what you've foreseen."
('Where the crakeberries grow – Robert Graves gives an account of himself to Leslie Norris', *Listener*, 28 May 1970 http://www.lib.buy.edu/~english/wwwI/influence/graves.html (accessed 3 March, 2014)

Elsewhere he contends:

> I have held hitherto and still hold that Poetry is for the poet a means of informing himself on many planes simultaneously, the plane of primitive imagery, the intellectual plane, the musical plane of rhythm structure and texture – of informing himself on these and possibly on other distinguishable planes of the relation in his mind of certain inharmonious interests, you may call them his sub-personalities or other selves. (Graves 1923, 353)

The very term White Goddess points to an archetypal approach, and along with the emphasis on the poetic mind and its workings, they imply a psychoanalytic perspective. Graves though, did not hold psychoanalysis in the highest esteem and Jungian psychology had no conscious influence in the concept of the Goddess (Day 1963, 165). In fact, he refused to take Jung seriously and referred to him with sarcasm and, one might argue, contempt (Seymour-Smith 1982, 401)[89] .

Graves is so firm and positive about the chimeric nature of what he has named the Goddess, that he leaves no room for scepticism and interrogation; "despite the possibility that she is illusory the poet's tone is perversely confident, even jubilant." (Kirkham 1969, 206) Indeed, he seems to rejoice in the liminality of the Goddess and the perpetual pursuit for her, and furthermore he considers them an essential quality of poetic activity. This joy of the chase of the illusory is the main component of the poet's attraction to her; Graves is attracted to the liminal (which he sees as a female quality par excellence) and to its pursuit. It is liminality per se that fascinates him, invigorating his poetic activity, and it is the very liminality of the Goddess that challenges the poetic mind and instigates creative activity. Yet, poetic endeavour is not condemned to a sterile, meaningless and repetitive pursuit: the search for the Goddess is itself a rewarding and progressive experience: "But I am gifted, even in November rawest of seasons", "I forget cruelty and past betrayal, careless of where the next bright bolt may fall." (Graves 1948, 5) The poet acknowledges the role of the Goddess in his poetic and creative activity and feels girded with the inspiration and creativity granted

[89] Snipes (1979, 25) mentions that although Graves despised Jungian psychology, especially as an approach to the White Goddess, it is this very approach which can account for his strong preoccupation with the White Goddess.

to him as a reward for his quest and as a result of his will and bold determination to scorn "God Apollo's golden mean" and seek her "in the volcano's head".

> Graves's system is a *paysage moralisé*, rather than a landscape from which nymphs and value have departed…
>
> But as the landscape of his mind given a habitation and a name, the world of the Goddess is at once distanced from Graves and only his own. He can roam through it as a man of property, or as an explorer, or as a culture hero calling things into existence by giving them names. (Stade 1967, 40)

Constant pursuit of the Muse is what determines the poetic mind and defines the poet. A true poet never relaxes or feels a sense of conquest and achievement but always seeks the Muse while knowing he can never conquer or possess her. This pursuit of liminality is the endless dialectical process of the poetic mind while creating and articulating poetry.

The pursuit and adoration of the Muse is not restricted to the poet's wife, mistress or a woman he is secretly in love with. The distinction between the Goddess as such and the individual woman that may occasionally incarnate and personify her is made by Graves himself:

> But the real, perpetually obsessed Muse-poet makes a distinction between the Goddess as revealed in the supreme power, glory, wisdom and love of woman, and the individual woman in whom the Goddess may take up residence for a month, a year, seven years, or even longer. The Goddess abides; and it may be that he will again have knowledge of her through his experience of another woman. (Graves 1997, 832)

The poet-Muse relationship goes beyond the conventional romantic love which merely metaphorizes the poet's attraction towards the Goddess and his pursuit of her:

> A poet's absolute love, his readiness to trust in woman's wisdom, whatever may ensue, represents a nostalgia for human truth. He does not, however, love indiscriminately, but only *the* woman, the royal woman, an incarnation of the Goddess, gifted with her *kra*, who (he assures himself) is waiting somewhere to restore the lost mysteries of mankind. (Graves 1962, 63)[90]

The poet's "absolute love" for the Goddess reflects his absolute love for truth. This "perpetual other woman" to whom he is eternally devoted, is, like truth and knowledge, a vision and at the same time a reality. She is the

---

[90] *Kra* is a term borrowed from West African culture connoting a supernatural power (Graves 1962, 57-65).

challenge that every poet should face and she incorporates all the abstraction and, at the same time, all the reality that a challenge involves. The terms "unknown Muse" and "perpetual other woman" suggest her a priori existence, defiant of a fixed identity, and the continuity inherent in the poet's quest. Graves further attributes a spiritual quality to the Goddess/Muse-poet relationship:

> The poet-Muse relationship can never be a domestic one, nor need it be sexually consummated; since, despite all the symptoms of romantic love, it belongs to another order of experience – which, for want of a better term, we must call "spiritual." (Graves 1965, 44)

This is an advocation of an experience that transcends the limits of a conventional relationship between a poet and his real or imaginary Muse and which "despite all the symptoms of romantic love" encompasses the intellectual and spiritual realms.

One of the most interesting ideas in the poem "In Dedication" is the emphasis on the personal and totally individual nature of the poet's quest for the White Goddess as an aspect of Graves's idiosyncratic approach to poetry and creativity (Carter 1989, 4). He embarks on a conscious, determined search for her, "I sailed to find her", "seeking her", which is his own poetic pilgrimage and his own existential and spiritual quest: "Whom I desired above all things to know." The poet demonstrates an awareness of the risks and the obstacles that such a quest involves, since the objective of his search is to encounter an entity that is to be sought "at the volcano's head, among pack ice, or where the track had faded beyond the cavern of the seven sleepers." He has already admitted to the intangible and abstract nature of the Goddess, "sister of the mirage and echo" who dwells "in distant regions likeliest to hold her", yet he is determined to "go my headstrong and heroic way." With the White Goddess, Robert Graves introduces a poetic theory which is not simply a critical discourse or a manifesto declaring a new thematic or technical approach to poetry, but a serious consideration of poetry, an investigation of poetic activity and an instructive heritage to poets of the future. The significance of this perspective does not lie merely in the pursuit and role of the Muse, an ancient literary topos, but in the emphasis on poetic consciousness and, more particularly, in its processes, its potential and its dynamics. The poem "In Dedication" is an intellectual, premeditated declaration of the poet's alliance with a force permeating and determining every single poetic utterance of his and every aspect of his poetic activity whether this takes place in his mind or on the page.

Another component of the experience of the White Goddess, inextricably linked to liminality, is that of the poetic trance. Graves describes the personal, magical experience of the liminality of the White Goddess as a trance in which the poet finds himself while writing a poem. This trance however is not of the kind that one experiences while under the influence of any type of drug. Having experienced both a drug-induced trance and a Muse-induced one, Graves concludes: "A mushroom trance is relatively passive; a poetic trance, active – the pen running briskly across paper." (Graves 1962, 128)[91] According to him, while the poetic trance differs significantly from the drug-induced trance, it is very similar to the religious trance:

> Religious ecstasy and the poetic trance, if one looks at these phenomena subjectively, are both achieved by divine inspiration; or if looked at objectively, by self-hypnosis. Religious ecstasy is invited by prayers, music, and solemn ritual. Formalities of verse-printing invite the poetic trance: which means, for instance, that a sonnet printed as a prose paragraph will be extremely hard to read as a poem. Prose intelligence operates on one level only; poetic intelligence operates in depth, as if under narcotics, with all its five inner senses alert. (Graves 1967, 156)

The "as if" element that relates the poetic trance with the drug-induced trance does not bring the two experiences closer together but on the contrary highlights their fundamental difference, which lies in the alertness of the mind and the cognitive processes. The poetic trance resembles only metaphorically the narcotic trance since, according to Graves, the latter is the best way to describe the former in an intelligible manner.

Elsewhere Graves explains that "Symptoms of the trance in which poetic composition occurs differ greatly from those of an induced mediumistic trance; though both seem directed by an external power" and he further clarifies that "The writing is not 'automatic', as in a mediumistic trance when the pen travels without pause over the paper, but is broken by frequent critical amendments and excisions." (Graves 1965, 42-43) In other words, he is suggesting a state of subliminal, transcendental mental activity and not one of a frenzied hyperactivity as is common when under the influence of drugs. The trance therefore, which the pilgrimage to the White Goddess involves, does not result in arbitrary utterances of a surrealistic stream of consciousness. While Graves acknowledges both the significance and contribution of the unconscious in the creative process – "A true poem is

---

[91] While in America in 1960, Graves experienced a hallucinogenic trance when he took a natural herb used by indigenous Mexicans. It was this experience that enabled him to distinguish between the poetic and drug-induced trance (Graves 1962, 111-129).

best regarded as already existing before it has been composed" (ibid., 74) namely, it exists in a seminal form in the mind of the poet – still he does not dismiss or underestimate the importance of discipline, composition and structure in poetry "Poetry does not deny the intellect, or the discipline of reason but transcends both." (Graves 1962, 81) The kind of trance that he is suggesting is neither the result of cultural or collective conditioning nor the effect of a self-inflicted transcendence. It is not the kind of trance that involves disassociation from or dispossession of one's self but on the contrary it is a revisiting of one's self. It is not about the loss of control but about distilled emotions and about intuitive thought and measure.

Graves distinguishes between different levels of trance according to the degree of disengagement from the external environment and the critical faculty of the poet's mind (Graves 1949, 1). Once the state of trance has terminated the poet proceeds with the revision of his work, which will depend on the degree of the trance: a poem written during a light trance will not require much revision while a poem produced under a state of severe trance will require a great amount of revision and correction mostly in its technical aspects. "After the initial rush of expression comes critical appraisal and meticulous rewriting, where all the poet's craft is put to the service of the unique requirements of this particular poem. Graves says he writes approximately ten drafts of a poem." (Snipes 1979, 15)

The Gravesian poetic trance involves intense mental activity and constitutes an awakening of the poetic mind:

> The trance operates in a "reasonable" way but not in the rational mode: in this trance, which is "the lightest form of sleep, a form in which you can think in a reasonable way and, at the same time, you can dredge up from your memory all the words and images you don't know you know. (Kohli 1974, 103)

Graves's apprehension of the poetic trance as a component of the poet's personal experience of the White Goddess is explicit yet quite complex since it is based on this peculiar combination of inspiration and discipline, of the sublime and the mundane.

The poetic trance is further permeated by the concept of *baraka,* discussed extensively in *The Oxford Addresses on Poetry*.[92] The word itself means "lightning" or "divine rupture" and its subsequent religious usage suggests a blessedness or a holy spell.

---

[92] In *The Oxford Addresses on Poetry* Graves mentions that Arab villagers believe that objects possess their own baraka, namely their inherent particular quality which makes them unique (Graves 1962, 99-107).

> Since lightning is a phenomenon everywhere attributed to the gods, baraka means the sudden divine rapture which overcomes either a prophet or a group of fervent devotees (Dervish dancers, for example, or the primitive Christians at the Feast of Pentecost) whom it unites in a bond of love: it can therefore stand for the blessedness acquired by holy shrines and other places where the spirit of God has been plainly manifested. (Graves 1962, 99)

This state of rapture allows the mind and the senses to operate fully and does not numb them. Graves's argument concerning baraka is that "*Baraka* in literature and the creative arts is of the utmost importance. Remember that it originally meant 'divine inspiration' or 'blessedness' – a quality which the most daring intellectual experiments, or works most shrewdly designed for the current market, cannot possess." (ibid., 102) Baraka is the blessed instant during the interaction between the Muse and the poet, the moment when "true" poetry occurs. It is the point of culmination of this interaction and an apotheosis of the poetic mind. Versification is not only the result but also the occasion for trance and the state of baraka, an initiation to the inner dialogue between poet and Muse, in fact a dialogue of the poet with himself or as Graves puts it "a private message to himself from himself." (Graves 1949, 1) Undoubtedly, this dialectic quality defines Gravesian poetic activity:

> This is a close enough metaphor for Poetry. The source of light strikes the first mirror, which is that of immediate sensuous perception; the image is reflected in a second mirror, a more epicritic one: and if one accepts the view that every person has various degrees of consciousness corresponding to the Classical seven degrees of hypnosis, into which the poet's mind descends during the composition of a Muse poem, it is fair to say that the extraordinary complex patterns of such a poem are eventually derived from the first pure illumination of the poet's mirror. It is the *angle* at which the mirrors are set that determines the final result. (Graves 1967, 156)

The metaphor of the light reflected in a series of mirrors illustrates the idea of baraka and the poetic trance in its totality. The light striking the first mirror corresponds to the "sudden divine rupture" that signifies the state of baraka. The subsequent reflection on different mirrors, "more epicritic" ones, corresponds to the different levels of trance which involve various degrees of engagement of the poet's critical faculty. The final product of this process of refinement is an amended and ameliorated extract of the very "first pure illumination of the poet's mirror", namely the moment of poetic epiphany and inspiration, the state of baraka.

The state of trance is described by Graves as a magical one but not of the kind which implies magic as an occultist practice: "Magic is a poetic, not a scientific term." (Graves 1965, 31). Commenting on the poem "Witches", John Vickery points out:

> The interesting thematic feature of this poem is Graves's argument that magic is real and true just as love is and that lack of belief in either is a sign of limited intelligence which brings its own punishment. This is not to say that he views magic in the manner of Aleister Crowley, of Charles Williams, or even William Butler Yeats. Rather magic seems to be associated with individually and personally induced imaginative experiences, with the mind's capacity to invest or remember situations that it is not now witnessing. (Vickery 1972, 21)

The Gravesian notion of magic pertains to a mental, psychological and esoteric experience: "There is no cabalistic or occult element in such poet-Muse relationships, however difficult they may be to achieve and maintain." (Graves 1962, 78-79) Magic seems to connote more of a deep memory and a prolific imagination.

> Yet for all his belief in the goddess and in her magic, it is obvious that what Graves is talking about is not a theologically conceived meta-human "external spiritual authority", but rather a factor in the structure of the poetic personality. (Seymour-Smith 1982, 401)

In short, the pilgrimage to the White Goddess is a unique individual experience of the poet, and of every person who thinks in poetic terms, which involves a peculiar synergy of reason and vision. This experience is neither rational (as we conventionally understand and use the word) nor irrational but, as I would like to call it, *suprarational*. Graves himself has used a similar word in "The Dedicated Poet" where he illustrates the example of a poet who follows the Muse and not the Apollonian way of writing poetry:

> Muse poetry is composed at the back of the mind: an unaccountable product of a trance in which the emotions of love, fear, anger, or grief are profoundly engaged though at the same time powerfully disciplined; in which intuitive thought reigns supralogically, and personal rhythm subdues metre to its purposes. (Graves 1962, 10)

The significance of his proposal and theory is that it provides a new approach to the ideas of trance, ecstasy, inspiration, in relation not only to poetry but to creativity in general. "For Graves, a poem must make sense; deliberate obscurity is an affectation. (Graves condemns Ezra Pound on this score.) But the poem must begin 'beyond reason' in inspiration, welling up from the poetic trance." (Snipes 1979, 15) Poetic creativity is a perennial interaction, a dialogue taking place in poetic consciousness. The liminal White Goddess can be considered an epitome of poetic consciousness and is therefore a transcendental concept.

The notion of magic as a part and a prerequisite of the experience of the White Goddess is neither that of a mystical cult nor of a religious practice. Magic connotes the imaginative and the creative as opposed to the sterile Apollonian way followed by "all sober men" and "all saints". In short, the White Goddess is an articulation of the poet's mental and esoteric experience and a declaration of the boundless and infinite powers of poetic inspiration. "*The White Goddess* in its wayward exposition of his own deepest experience tells of a new freedom and new source of power." (Cohen 1963, 97)

This view of poetry and creativity, while providing a challenging and unique discourse, can raise serious concerns regarding its very idiosyncratic nature. This purely Gravesian system and theory may prove inadequate or arbitrary as a comprehensive poetic theory on the basis of being too personal. The concept of trance raises the legitimate question of whether it applies to all poets and whether Graves is not overambitious or even vain in assuming the applicability of his theory to all poets. Powell calls *The White Goddess* "a remarkable if oblique insight into that idiosyncratic, packed intelligence which underlies even Graves' most modest poems." (Powell 1997, 89) Indeed the idiosyncratic nature of the White Goddess manifests the intellectual seclusion which to a great extent characterizes Graves's work and is reflected in his geographical and intellectual distancing from the cultural and literary milieu of his times. This personal system in conjunction with Graves's intellectual isolation can be seen as a rebellion against the cultural establishment of British belle lettres and in particular as a defiance of the contemporary modernist scene (O'Prey 2001, 42).

I believe that Graves should be solely seen as a sui generis poet and intellectual and his work as a distinct intellectual and poetic statement. His entire corpus reveals a very particular outlook on poetry and creativity in general. As Steiner points out:

> Behind the poems, the novels, the critical essays, the translations and the volumes of anthropology and myth, lies a central vision, a unified image of reality and poetic experience toward which the individual creations contribute as stones to a mosaic. (Steiner 1960, 343)

Indeed, every poet who articulates his ideas and experience of being a poet does so from a personal perspective. The difference in Graves's case is this subtle amalgamation of the mythical, the poetic, the trivial, the transcendental and the liminal, all of which contribute to the composition of this large and versatile mosaic that his entire oeuvre is. What, undoubtedly, deserves the admiration of even his critics is the consistency and resolution that distinguishes his poetic discourse, as well as the zest and genuineness of his attitude towards poetry: these have enabled the White Goddess to exercise a strong and lasting effect on the theory as well as the practice of poetry:

> Graves has had a salubrious effect upon poetry, insisting upon both inspiration and craftsmanship, ridiculing cliché and insincerity, promoting a meticulous study of the meanings and emotional overtones of words. These values will surely always be valid. Moreover, for the 'now' generation, he demonstrates that even the remote past may impart some unique wisdom to the perceptive mind. (Snipes 1979, 25)

The inextricable link between female liminality and poetic articulation, which constitutes the very essence of the conception of White Goddess, is Graves's major contribution to the literary world. This same link can be found in Idwar al-Kharrat's *City of Saffron* and *Girls of Alexandria*,[93] two novels verging on autobiography, stream of consciousness and diary without being any one of these three exclusively. In the following pages I shall explore the relationship between female liminality and poetic utterance in these two novels and illustrate how the hero/narrator epitomizes the Gravesian poet who interacts with the White Goddess (incarnated in the various Alexandrian women he encounters) and partakes in its experience through literary articulation.[94] Women in both novels are strongly related to his sexual and adult awakening: through their bodies and their physical existence they become vehicles for the perennial mysteries of life, and mostly for the mysterious link between sexuality, life and death, where sex and sexuality signify life and defiance of death. Yet, women in these two novels are not seen as sexual objects or mere vehicles for erotic desire:

---

[93] The original title of *City of Saffron* is *Turabuha Za'faran* which literally translates into *Her earth is saffron* while the original title of *Girls of Alexandria* is *Ya banat Iskandariya* which translates into *Oh Girls of Alexandria*, an exclamation but also an invocation to the women of Alexandria, the author's source of inspiration and creative niche.

[94] In both novels the dividing lines between the narrator and the hero are continuously blurred, often resulting in confusion as to who is speaking. Furthermore, because both novels are to a great extent autobiographical there is always an underlying impression that it is the author himself who is speaking. In this part of the Chapter I shall be referring to the hero/narrator without touching upon the narratological issue of the fusion between author, hero and narrator as this does not fall within the objectives of my discussion.

though dwelling on their physical attributes in a highly descriptive manner, al-Kharrat manages to depart from pure physicality and delves into the mysterious and metaphysical implications of female liminality. For the purposes of my discussion, I shall concentrate on the female characters of Hosniya, Rana and the silent Madonna of Ghobrial.

The titles suggest two novels on Alexandria, the author's beloved city and creative niche. The city of Alexandria can therefore be considered as the theme of both books though alternatively the erotic initiation of a young boy could be considered as the main theme in these two novels which are a peculiar combination of memories, fantasies, dreams, thoughts, incantations and poetic utterances.[95] Indeed both novels operate on a multithematic level, yet the common denominator in both of them is the presence of women who feature in every Chapter and occupy the major part of the hero/narrator's conscious and unconscious world. Al-Kharrat focuses on women and their function in the hero's/narrator's daily, emotional, mental and creative life. The magical journey to the hero/narrator's inner world originates in the streets of Alexandria and in the women who inhabit the city. It starts in *City of Saffron* and continues in the second book, *Girls of Alexandria*, a title which suggests more explicitly that inextricable link between the hero/narrator, his city and the women in it. *Girls of Alexandria* follows the same style as *City of Saffron*, fusing naturalism and modernism, prose and poetry, reality and fantasy, past and present, the conscious and the unconscious. Eventually in both books, Alexandria becomes its women which in turn signify the hero/narrator's mental, emotional, creative and existential identity.

> Alexandria for me is a metaphysical condition, an adventure in spirit to comprehend an inner truth, a confrontation and an identification with the absolute and with the otherness that extends limitlessly on the face of a turbulent or quiescent sea toward an ambiguous horizon. (Al-Kharrat 1998, 16)

The phrase "metaphysical condition" encapsulates not only Al-Kharrat's but also the narrator/hero's predicament. It is an internal quest of an esoteric

---

[95] An element that is greatly responsible for the overriding significance of the initiation theme is the highly sensual descriptions by Al-Kharrat and the often exaggerated style. Stefan Mayer consents to the nearly obsessional nature of Al-Kharrat's descriptions which he attributes to the transcendental narrative style that the author has adopted in order to articulate issues of gender and sexuality. Mayer contextualizes his argument through the dialectics of form and content. See Stefan G. Mayer, *The Experimental Arabic Novel, Postcolonial Literary Modernism in the Levant*, (New York: State University of New York Press, 2001, 209-213)

nature, an "adventure in spirit", a self-quest in order to discover and obtain "an inner truth". Nonetheless, this quest echoes the Gravesian quest for the White Goddess which is in essence the "nostalgia for human truth" (Graves 1962, 63). Indeed both Graves and Al-Kharrat, each in his own idiosyncratic way, communicate the inextricable link between female liminality and literary activity through the constant pursuit of what the former calls the White Goddess and the latter Alexandria. They both try to describe this "metaphysical condition" which is nothing else than the condition of being a poet. Al-Kharrat's Muse is Alexandria manifested in the sea and, most significantly, in the city's women. The search for an inner truth, epitomized in the city of Alexandria, occurs through the encounter with various women of the city and the significance they have for the hero/narrator. Eventually, Alexandria and its women become the "will to truth" which Keane sees behind the quest for the Gravesian White Goddess. The amalgamation of the city, its women and the author constitutes the backbone of the most significant notion in both books, namely female liminality and poetic utterance.

> Kharrat's narrative is robust, emotive, expansive, spontaneous, and lyrical. He paints a panorama. In his memory, he roams throughout Alexandria, and the women he remembers represent a connective thread of experience that unifies and distils for him the essence of the city, and of his own existence. (Meyer 2001, 211)

Women in both novels are not only the hero/narrator's centre of attention but they are also given an existential significance. More particularly, they signify his interaction with both the external world and his own internal world. They are an external instigation for a deeper delving into his internal world. Women in Al-Kharrat vacillate between the real and the imaginary, the physical and the abstract, the tangible and the intangible, the "here" and the "there". They vacillate between the external and the internal world of the hero/narrator without belonging to one of these worlds exclusively. They are not subject to fixation and constraints. In short, they are evanescent and liminal, and it is this very liminality that fascinates the hero/narrator and instigates the dialectic between his internal and external worlds.

Shimon Ballas (1993) points out that Al-Kharrat's heroes are trapped between a constricting exterior and a suffocating interior world:

> Al-Kharrat's protagonist is depicted as a wanderer between two worlds: the exterior world constricts him to the point of suffocation, and his interior world seals off all paths of communication. In other words, al-Kharrat's protagonists live within a closed circle with no exit from their predicament. They gaze at their surroundings in fear and repulsion and, carried away by

> their thoughts, increasingly absorbed by daydreams which alienate them further, they drift toward total detachment. (Ballas, 26)

This idea of entrapment is present in *City of Saffron* and in *Girls of Alexandria* where young Mikhail feels puzzled and restricted by his surrounding reality and often suffocated by his melancholic and depressed interior world. However, unlike other works by Al-Kharrat – to which Ballas refers - in these two novels there is an exit from the hero's predicament. The escape for him are the women who constitute the link with the external world but they also signify a new route in his troubled internal world. Women are Mikhail's bridge to the world and most importantly to himself. This new route, this bridge instigates his creativity and liberates him from the "closed circle" he is in. For young Mikhail, women are a way of self-realization. They seem to be a distant "other", yet they form a large part of his mental and emotional world; he has an esoteric relationship with them as the Gravesian poet has with the Muse.

City of Saffron introduces female liminality through Hosniya, the first female character to appear in the novel, who is young Mikhail's neighbour and to whom he is very much attracted.

> She was thin. She had jet-black hair bound in a white kerchief.
> She was small, and older than me by perhaps only a couple of years. Something about her I liked a lot; it greatly attracted me. (al-Kharrat 1989, 4)

Hosniya is presented in the novel in terms of her physicality which is rendered in a sensuous and sexually implicit manner:

> She sat in a wicker chair, beside a large round marble table spread with a white open-work cloth. Her nightshift, while loose on her, did not reach to her knees. She sat with her legs apart, stretching them out before her in a languid fatigue. …I saw her eyes, wide in her sharp, bony face. They looked puffy, and her eyebrows were very arched and thin above the socket. (ibid.)

The emphasis on Hosniya's physical attributes points clearly to her sexuality: the "sharp bony face", the "wide" and "puffy" eyes, the eyebrows "very arched and thin above the socket", the "languid fatigue", and the stretched parted legs are indicators of a sexually loaded atmosphere and of an underlying eroticism which is accentuated by Mikhail's agitation and embarrassment whenever he encounters her.

> At first Hosniya would merely nod her head at me by way of greeting; and I would run away up the stairs, feeling the blood rush to my face, uncertain whether I had returned the greeting or simply fled. (ibid., 5)

Apart from these rather stylistically voyeuristic descriptions of Hosniya there is a very clear and more explicit reference to the sexual nature of Mikhail's perception and experience of her:

> Suddenly she put out a thin arm and drew my head close to her. My face was under her unbound breast; I could feel it, soft and firm and small, as she pressed my head against her thin flank, against the soft weave of her shift. (ibid.)

This scene is at first glance a typical rendition of a young boy's first close experience of women as Mikhail feels for the first time in his life the female breast, the perennial emblem of femininity. The "unbound", "soft and firm and small" breast which he feels against his body agitates and shocks him. "And then I fled from her, my head pounding as I took the stairs at a run." (ibid.) Unwittingly, Mikhail's mother underscores the aspect of liminality by mentioning the ghost, as she tries to account for her son's shock and puzzlement:

> My mother laughed as she opened the door. "What's the matter with you?" she cried. "Saw a ghost in broad daylight or something? Get in then, and wash your face – come on, come in." (ibid.)

Regardless of her strong physical presence and the intoxicating effects that her body and sexuality have on Mikhail, Hosniya is intangible and elusive.

> I loved her, but I was afraid of something intangible in her, latent in the languor of her thin and debilitated frame.
>
> Once she said to me, avoiding my gaze, that she traveled at night; that she went very far away, and that these night journeys were very tiring, and that the sun never shone then. I imagined that I understood perfectly, and that perhaps she went to the Cairo railway station and spent the night travelling in the train, returning before morning. I believed that, and I knew at the same time that she never left the house. (ibid., 6)

The significance of Hosniya's journey, apart from being a metaphor for her prostitution, is the affirmation of her itinerant and liminal nature. Hosniya never leaves her house yet she is travelling (whether to Cairo railway station or to a fictitious location where "the sun never shone" is not of major importance) and Mikhail's firm belief in this paradox consents to its validity. Mikhail does not resemble the other boys of his age who, in the midst of puberty, are attracted to female physicality in its basic, and carnal dimension: he is able to perceive women beyond that level and is attracted to the invisible, intangible qualities of femininity and in particular to liminality. Mikhail is the perennial poet, in fact, the Gravesian poet with a specific outlook on life: he is the perceptive one who is susceptible to the abstract and the metaphysical and, as such, he perceives women in their multiple and variegated nature.[96] It is not his naiveté which makes him believe in Hosniya's night journeys but his intuition and his susceptibility to the perception of things numinous, hidden "in the languor of her thin and debilitated frame." The thin and debilitated frame exercises a strong attraction upon Mikhail and at the same time it frightens him. It is this paradoxical and peculiar coexistence of concreteness and abstraction, of presence and absence, of reality and fantasy which attracts and simultaneously daunts the young hero. It is this very combination that determines his perception of women and his relationship to them. Mikhail's attraction to Hosniya echoes the Gravesian poetic attraction to the Goddess who is physical ("whose eyes were blue, with rowan-berry lips, with hair curled honey-coloured to white hips") but who is also impersonal and evanescent ("in distant regions likeliest to hold her"). Hosniya travels "very far away" in her own distant regions where Mikhail cannot reach her. Like the Goddess's distant regions, Hosniya's are psychic and esoteric. Mikhail's poetic susceptibility to abstract and metaphysical experiences enables him to perceive the liminality of the young girl. This combination of physicality and intangibility, which cannot be fully comprehended and possessed, constitutes Mikhail's perception of Hosniya. And as a true Gravesian poet he is intrigued and fascinated by this liminality.

The fact that Hosniya is a prostitute emphasizes her liminal nature. She belongs to all men and to none of them at the same time. Anybody can "have" her in a strictly carnal sense but nobody can actually possess her, nobody can possess her sexuality and her spirit. Every night she embarks on her journey to her own distant regions. The timing of the journeys is not at all accidental: during those very moments of her physical possession by her

---

[96] Mikhail's susceptibility to the abstract and the metaphysical conforms to the Bildungs/Künstlerroman hero such as Tonio in Thomas Mann's *Tonio Kröger* and Stephen in James Joyce's *A Portrait of the Artist as a Young Man*. However, while Tonio and Stephen try to establish an identity within a particular socio-historical and cultural context, Mikhail, though an integral and active part of his cultural, historical and religious milieu, is not at odds with it. Furthermore, he claims no uniqueness as is common with the Bildungs/Künstlerroman hero and he does not follow a linear development as a character.

customers Hosniya is embarking on her journey to the unknown. This is the very moment where her liminality is being asserted and accentuated. The journeys she undertakes are "very tiring" and the sun never shines while they are taking place, a clear reference to the gloomy, sad and nocturnal nature of her profession. Yet, the absence of the sun also implies the lunar and obscure elements inherent in liminality.

Al-Kharrat is not willing to dwell on the significance of Hosniya in Mikhail's initiation to sexuality and adulthood. This is particularly evident in the scene where she hides from the police and seeks shelter in Mikhail's house. Mikhail's father puts her in the same bed with his children so Hosniya lies next to Mikhail who is supposedly asleep and he feels her cold body trembling from fear. Hosniya's physicality assumes a secondary role to the "something intangible" which the young hero/narrator perceives in her and which exercises an immense attraction on him. It is the mystery that surrounds her which attracts Mikhail and also puzzles him, and the fact that she is close to him but distant at the same time. Her sudden departure from his life reinforces this distance and mystery, and gives her a subliminal, almost sacred, quality. Mikhail has a dream/fantasy in which the cart that carried Hosniya and her mother with their belongings is "blown and scattered to the winds." (al-Kharrat 1989, 13) Hosniya falls under the hoofs of the cart horses: "Her eyes turn towards me from the ground, hard flowing from them a wordless tenderness I do not want" (ibid.). Mikhail assumes a Christ-like appearance and embraces her in a gesture of salvation and love. "I embrace her with hands pierced by nails, my side stabbed by a lance; and seeping from my wound, a few drops of blood." (ibid.) The allusion to Christianity adds a further spiritual nuance to the relationship between Hosniya and Mikhail. Mikhail's sacrificial gesture for the sake of Hosniya strongly resonates with the sacrifice of the Gravesian poet for the sake of the Goddess.

Hosniya reappears in Chapter Four of *City of Saffron* confirming Mikhail's belief that she is omnipresent while still absent. In this Chapter the older boys in Mikhail's school share with the younger ones their first sexual experiences. One of the older boys, Ghurrayib, recounts his experience with a prostitute named Hosniya who did not accept money from him because he lived in el-Kurum street and she told him that she also used to live there and she wanted to return a debt she had to some kind neighbours there. Ghurrayib describes her as "thin and dark, and sort of heated-up, like fire – and nice, as well." (ibid., 59) However, he also refers to her in a highly derogatory and humiliating manner:

> He said that whatever, or whoever she was, she was a prostitute, the bitch, and that he was going to go back to her and give her the money with a kick up the backside, and belt her if she opened her mouth. (ibid.)

Mikhail listens to these comments "in turmoil" and with his "heart stricken", unable to believe "it was her at all." (ibid.) For him Hosniya is not a contemptible prostitute but his beloved neighbour with the "debilitated frame" and with "something intangible in her", a mysterious and elusive girl. The contrast between Mikhail and the other boys confirms the distinctive poetic nature which goes beyond ordinary perception and operates on an altogether subliminal level. Mikhail here epitomizes the perennial poet who possesses a subtle perception and sees in Hosniya not profanity and disgrace but the femininity and liminality which attract and intrigue him.

In this same Chapter, titled "A Vessel Borne on the Body's Flood-tide", Mikhail experiences his first true sexual awakening yet not with a prostitute or a promiscuous woman as happened with all his friends. Mikhail reads the *Arabian Nights* and through the fascinating descriptions and the sensuous references to sexuality and lust he realizes the arousal of his sexuality and the birth of his sexual self. Shehrazad, the woman poet, the woman creator fascinates him and excites not only his senses but also his imagination:

> And the church bells of the clock pealed out, and for the first time the world became bright with the fire of knowledge and the flood gushed out; and I became a vessel afloat, borne on the flood-tide; and there is no road through the roaring waves of these high seas, where I rise and fall to this day. (ibid., 65)

Indeed, Mikhail conforms to the Gravesian definition of the poet as "someone who lives and thinks in a certain way" (Graves, 1970) and who practises poetry as "a way of being and thinking" (Graves 1967, 155). Al-Kharrat elevates his hero even further by ascribing to him a refined and sublime perception of a very physical experience which is the bodily awakening of a young boy's sexuality. Even such a physical experience is associated with knowledge and truth: "the world became bright with the fire of knowledge and the flood gushed out." (al-Kharrat 1989, 65) The references to water (flood, afloat, flood-tide, roaring waves, high seas) are suggestive of the sexual awakening but they also signify the awakening of imagination and creativity. Water, associated with cosmic creation and the origins of life,[97] becomes a metaphor for poetic creation. The newly born

---

[97] This is particularly true in Egyptian mythology where Nun is a deity symbolizing water.

"vessel afloat" is not Mikhail's body but primarily his mind and spirit which embark on a journey to creativity. The character of Hosniya signifies Mikhail's first experience of female liminality and establishes his attraction towards it.

In Chapter Three Mikhail encounters another version of female immanence and liminality through Rana, the owner of "Rana's Hotel" by the sea where his uncle stays. As in the case of Hosniya, it is physical description and sexuality that initially prevail as Mikhail suddenly enters his uncle's room after Rana and his uncle have just had sex.

> Her full, round breasts trembled under the soft material; and the part which showed in the wide opening of the gown glistened with sweat.
>
> I managed not to cry as she pulled me by the hand to sit down beside her on the bed; obeying her, I felt her hot flesh through the gown which gaped open between the buttons – at her breasts, and the middle of her stomach, and between her legs; it was buttoned with big shiny round buttons made of white mother-of-pearl. Her body was luxurious and gratuitously offered. (ibid., 36-37)

This time there is a stronger emphasis on sexuality in a more explicit and naturalistic manner. The description of Rana is the description of a woman in her sexual and procreative role, immediately after copulation. The trembling breasts and the glistening sweat are illustrations of the procreative role of Rana. This highly voyeuristic, in style, description of her (indeed much more voyeuristic than Hosniya's) might seem exaggerated yet it should be remembered that Mikhail, in this particular chapter, is only a child and, as such, he possesses all the instinctive curiosity that surrounds anything related to the opposite sex, copulation, sexuality. This natural curiosity accounts for the exaggerated descriptions in this particular scene, and also for the frequent references to the female body in both novels. Al-Kharrat's descriptions are always detailed irrespective of their object. As S. Meyer (2001, 210) points out, al-Kharrat's descriptions of women in certain passages "are lovingly sensual, yet they also border on obsessional." These obsessive descriptions are neither pejorative nor profane but they correspond to the "nakedly worn magnificence" that Graves attributes to his White Goddess, indeed the magnificence of female sexuality "luxurious and gratuitously offered". Bodily grandeur and the procreative role are exactly what Mikhail notices in Rana and what puzzles and shocks him.

Rana has a strong effect on young Mikhail, and evokes a mixture of feelings in him. She intoxicates him through her femininity when "she puts her soft bare arms around my shoulders and squeezes me a bit, and looks down at me with her big eyes whose dark greenness trembles and overflows with a womanly tenderness which fills my heart" (al-Kharrat 1989, 35). Once again the author departs from the physical and sexual to encompass the emotional, the abstract and the intangible. Despite the initial shock and apprehension, and despite his repulsion over the scene he has just witnessed (manifested in his stubborn refusal to accept the chocolate from Rana), there is an overall joy at the encounter with another version of femininity although this time it is an encounter with the purely physical aspect of femininity within the context of copulation and procreative power. A sense of safety and contentment, confirming his unmistakable attraction to femininity, emanates from the womanly tenderness which fills his heart. Yet this tenderness emanates not only from Rana's body, but also from her eyes whose dark greenness trembles and exudes warmth and safety, echoing the transcendental feeling of the Gravesian narrator who feels "gifted even in November." "I caught a whiff of her secret smell and my face flamed." (al-Kharrat 1989, 36) While, in the case of Hosniya, Mikhail's attraction towards her had the typical characteristics of the attraction of a young boy towards a girl (he is attracted to her facial as well as her bodily features), in the case of Rana there is no such attraction. Although Mikhail observes the opening of the gown and the "full round breasts" (ibid.,) he is not sexually attracted in the way that an adult male would be and he does not want to sit near Rana. The attraction he has for her is of a different nature: it is the attraction to femininity per se which at that particular time in Mikhail's life is incarnated in Rana. She is just another manifestation of femininity: she is "the individual woman in whom the Goddess may take up residence for a month, a year, seven years, or even longer" (Graves 1958, 69).

Then Rana, just like Hosniya, vanishes; this time it is death that takes her away signifying her departure from the material and mundane world. She is, however, always present and immanent as a part of Mikhail's consciousness. She becomes an integral part of his memory and therefore eternal and liminal. Her existence is affirmed through his memory and consciousness:

> She was swimming beneath the window. She was wearing a pale-blue costume which clung to her, shining under the light ripple of the wave which washed over it and then gently washed away again. Her arms glided smoothly through the water, hardly stirring up a froth. Then I knew who she was.
>
> Rana. Rana whom I'd forgotten about. Her fresh young golden body could hardly contain the womanhood which bloomed and flowered, the first fruits of her fullness. She was younger than I knew her by far, a girl yet, and she had all the grace of a fish in the water. (al-Kharrat 1989, 45-46)

Rana is omnipresent in Mikhail's life, ostensibly real and tangible but in fact distant and intangible. She appears in the sea looking just as she was when alive, but this is only an emanation of her in the image of a woman in the sea. Rana exists in Mikhail's mind as an eternal figure transcending not only time but also her own personal identity: she can be any other woman in his life, any woman that he has met in the past and even any woman from his future. She undoubtedly assumes the qualities of the Gravesian White Goddess: she is unattainable just like the waves and the sea, she transcends time and identity. She is the "perennial other woman" to whom the Gravesian poet is attracted, precisely because she is always this other woman and therefore unattainable. The notions of eternity and liminality are rendered in the image of the sea and the waves. The sea, a traditionally female element, epitomizes the unmeasured and the liminal. The repetitive movements of the waves which washed over Rana's swimming costume and "then gently washed away again" signify and affirm the eternity of the sea and become a metaphor for this perennial "other" which is the sea and the White Goddess:

> My heart pounded and then stopped; who was she? Was she a younger sister whom I had not seen before? I was sure that it was her – *her*! Or was she the other whom I would love and lose? My eyes remained fixed on her, enchanted and distracted, and when she turned over on her back, floating on the water, I saw her round, golden-brown face, her eyes closed against the sun, floating towards me. (ibid., 46)

Though existing in the realm of fantasy and memory Rana is still as physical and as tangible as when Mikhail first met her in "Rana's Hotel". The excerpt above illustrates the fusion of the real and the imaginary, the tangible and the intangible, the physical and the mental, the present and the future. Rana's identity and existence becomes blurred: is she real or imaginary, is she somebody particular? She is "her", the real Rana who owned Rana's Hotel, and at the same time she is "*her*" the Rana that has become a part of Mikhail's consciousness, who is any woman from his past, present and future. Emma Westney Gaze (2000, 165) acknowledges an "omnitemporality" in al-Kharrat's *City of Saffron* and *Girls of Alexandria* which she argues is the narrative backbone of the two novels. Rana affirms this omnitemporality through her own transcendence of time and identity. Like the Gravesian Goddess she is the "perennial other woman", she is "*her*" in no need for any further descriptions and introductions. She exists in the poet's mind, real and imaginary at the same time. Again this fusion is what affects and attracts the hero/narrator: the familiar "intoxicating pungency" of the fragrance of her hair, the "gleaming fullness" of her cheeks. He is attracted to the immanence and liminality of Rana and he pledges an eternal love for this vague and obscure entity. The vagueness of her identity accentuates her liminality and her transience which is symbolized in the backward and forward movement of the sea and the waves.

> I knew that I would love her to the end of my life, a love like death, and my heart was the arena, the ocean floor for her fathomless boiling sea, her eternally surging waves which had no calmness in them. (al-Kharrat 1989, 46)

Once again the sea and the waves function as a metaphor for female liminality. The hero/narrator positions himself on the ocean floor, the arena which is emblematic of fixation and concreteness, whereas Rana is the fathomless boiling sea which signifies the boundless and immeasurable world of the White Goddess. The restless waves which come and go and are not subject to fixation and stability, represent the continuous search and journey of creation and inspiration. They also signify the chimeric nature of such a journey and they further communicate the Gravesian notion of creativity which entails the pursuit of the intangible. The metaphor of the arena renders the secret interaction, the struggle that characterizes this love for the liminal; the poet's mind is the battlefield, the meeting place of the Goddess and the poetic talent, it is the arena where an intense fight takes place. These two struggling forces engage in an intense interaction similar to copulation, a liminal act par excellence where both parties unite temporarily but can never actually obtain each other.

The sexual licentiousness of these women has no negative connotation. Their unrestrained erotic and sexual activity accentuates their defiance of fixation: while they offer their bodies unreservedly they can never be possessed or controlled in any other way. Furthermore, their intoxicating and whimsical quality verifies their kinship with the "sister of mirage and echo".

The women in *City of Saffron* are not merely the objects of the admiration or obsession of Mikhail, neither are they simply a window to the world of sexuality and eroticism. Both Hosniya and Rana are perceived by the hero/narrator in their physical and sexual dimension, yet they transcend their very physicality and sexuality, and encompass a subliminal and metaphysical realm by means of their mystery and liminality which in turn excites and inspires Mikhail. Most significantly, these two female characters exemplify the Gravesian White Goddess as the "perpetual other woman" in terms of her allure and the way she operates in the poet's mind and psyche.

It is not until Chapter Eight that al-Kharrat explicitly articulates the significance of female liminality for poetry and creation. This chapter contains a hymn to the females who appear in the novel and are known to Mikhail, but it is also a hymn to all women. Al-Kharrat chooses the letter *nun* (ن) of the Arabic alphabet as an emblem of femininity. This hymn is in fact a torrential articulation of the hero/narrator's mental and esoteric experience while in the state of inspiration and poetic utterance, in fact while under the influence of the Goddess:

> And I am ensconced in the niche of *your* nun, half of you to my right side a Fortune, an Ease enchanting, maddening, heavenly spasms; and half of you occulted the fettering rack, the lick of flames 'til the end of time. Both halves together my transport to Tantalus. My desire's fruit a Fate, drawing nigh to draw away once more. For you I yearn, I long, with my breast's whole inclination; and I am lean, consumed by care, my winding-sheet worn in the world between slumber and the lilting flute. Recanting I perjure myself; you blossom forth, and I shrink back; you grow in faith, and I break mine; my Doomsday you are. (ibid., 148)

The profound desire for the one woman who can also be any woman, carries a strong resonance of Graves's desire for the Muse who is "the perpetual other woman". The first two lines of the hymn suggest a clear reference to a comprehensive female figure. "My hymn to you, unique and precious one, anointed queen of the all-sufficing Ninth Day's kingdom; possessing all the eight day's clemency" (ibid., 147). Moreover, the "drawing nigh to draw away once more" echoes the chimeric White Goddess and the constant pursuit of the poet.

The letter nun (ن) which visually represents closure, womb and shelter is the symbol of female liminality in which the author makes his natural habitat and finds himself "ensconced" in the two halves. The round shape of the letter clearly suggests femininity and fertility. The location of the narrator within the nun signifies his comfort but also his entrapment; the nun is his Fortune and Ease but also his torment, his "fettering rack." He vacillates between the two while in search of an outlet.

The hymn represents the Gravesian poetic trance in which the poet is experiencing a hypnotic state while his senses are still alert and operating. It is a powerful and dramatic incantation with a strong sensual and emotional appeal but it is carefully composed and exhibits a clear control over words and language. The narrator addresses an entity to which he does not attribute a particular name but which assumes many identities: she is the "anointed queen", the "One Alone", Hosniya, Katrina, Iskandara, Haniya,

Ni`ma, Mona, Rana.[98] The highly descriptive and evocative diction ("I am ensconced in the niche of your nun", "The perne of desolation swooped down upon my shoulders") creates an intense and emotionally loaded mood. The hymn is an esoteric monologue which reveals aspects of the narrator's consciousness that are not revealed in any other part of the novel. It is an inner narrative which corresponds to the "private message" of the poet "to himself from himself" (Graves 1949, 1) and which Graves acknowledges as a part of the poetic trance. The hymn is written in italics partly as a way of formally distinguishing it from the rest of the text and partly to emphasize its unconventional and poetic nature. It begins with the reference to the many identities of the one woman, it then demonstrates the personal experience of the poet while under her influence and inspiration and concludes with a climactic ending which is the poetic, creative articulation. Indeed, it exemplifies the amalgamation of inspiration and skill that Robert Graves argues for.

The most significant part of the hymn is the final, climactic paragraph where the nun (ن) becomes a liberating agent for Mikhail and its utterance signifies his poetic epiphany:

> I inscribed the nun in drops of liquid silver upon a plaque of burning lead; I placed it in a vessel and rinsed it with rainwater, and, as the moon in her mansion spilled out her brilliance, I dipped my pen. And from the dim passageways of the sea the whales at once came to me, and my tongue was loosed, and I spoke new and eloquent conceits. Then I uttered the nun: the Number of the Power of the Names of her Letters, and a mighty light blazed forth, and there opened out to me heavenly ways to bliss. My inner being was filled with Knowledge; I recited strange prophecies; and all my pain was gone. (al-Kharrat 1989, 149)

There is nothing more Gravesian in this novel than this paragraph where the nun (ن) acts as a poetic catalyst. The liberation of the tongue and the recitation of prophecies signify the liberation of artistic and poetic activity. The inscription of the nun which subsequently leads to the utterance of "eloquent conceits" and eventually to the utterance of the *nun* itself corresponds to the idea of poetic nativity as Graves apprehends it and furthermore it resonates with the notion of creation in ancient Egyptian cosmogony as this is epitomized in the god of water and creation, Nun. The experience of the nun is in fact the experience of the White Goddess. Engagement with the Muse, the Goddess as an experience leads to "eloquent conceits" which communicate truth and purity. The "heavenly ways" to

---

[98] This is also a foreshadowing of the multiplicity of women that permeates *Girls of Alexandria.*

bliss and the filling with "Knowledge" is the enlightenment, the baraka that Graves associates with the state of the poet while under the influence of the Goddess. The narrator experiences a state of creative epiphany as his tongue is liberated and utters "new and eloquent conceits". He feels girded with a new power of inspiration precisely in the same manner that Graves feels "gifted, even in November / rawest of all seasons".

Another interesting kinship with Graves is the association of experience of the nun with knowledge ("My inner being was filled with Knowledge") which of course echoes the Gravesian "will to knowledge" as an integral part of the experience of the White Goddess. The moon that overlooks the narrator as he dips his pen in order to articulate his "eloquent conceits" corresponds to the White Goddess who "spilled out her brilliance" and enlightened the narrator.

In *Girls of Alexandria* the same notion of female liminality in relation to poetic articulation is an underlying theme. In the Preface of the novel Idwar al-Kharrat declares the strong attraction that the multiplicity and liminality of women have exercised on him. This multiplicity is illustrated through the superficial, brief references to the many girls of Alexandria, in contrast to *City of Saffron* where long sections are devoted to a specific woman. In *Girls of Alexandria* the effect is momentary yet it does not diminish the narrator's attraction to them.

> Girls of Alexandria, multiple, single, peerless: who are you? I have never met you face to face but I know you like a lover: and no one knows more than a lover. However many she is, she is one: however fleeting, she is eternal. How can I resist her? (al-Kharrat 1993, xiii)

This short Preface acknowledges explicitly the multiplicity and liminality of the women in the novel and the attraction that these two qualities exercise over the author. Emma Westney Gaze (2000, 266 and 270) points out that the women in *Girls of Alexandria* lose their individuality and become part of a general "you/she". It is precisely this multiplicity that attracts al-Kharrat and this mystery that tempts and challenges him: "However many she is, she is one." This is an echo of Graves's "perpetual other woman" and the "unknown Muse" who is mysterious and attractive because of her unknown identity and her lack of a fixed and identifiable existence:

> In the novel, however, the narrating protagonist, Mikhail, repeatedly cites an unnamed and ultimately unidentifiable feminine authority and mingles passages of her reported speech with passages of his own in an extended section of the novel's final chapter. While her 'she' remains distinct from his 'I' at any particular moment, their voices may be said to merge over the

> course of the entire section, when his words begin to appropriate images and sample sounds from hers. (Hammond 2000, 40)

This "unidentifiable feminine authority" whose voice merges with the voice of the hero/narrator is an inner part of him in the same manner as the White Goddess is a latent part of poetic consciousness. Al-Kharrat's "she" is the voice of the author's deepest layers of creative self, in a sense his creative anima, just as the Goddess is the poetic anima.

The figures of the silent Madonna of Ghobrial and Paola, the flirtatious tenant in Mikhail's house, which signify a fusion of sanctity and sexuality are both fleeting and irresistible. The silent Madonna of Ghobrial does not carry the Christian connotation that the reader would expect but she symbolizes transcendence and the different "order of experience" which Graves suggests as a catalyst in the poet-Muse relationship. She is a woman whom Mikhail encounters regularly on the way to school. He does not know anything about her, yet he is enchanted by her aura and appearance. This fascination with a completely strange woman is a repeated pattern in both of al-Kharrat's novels. Yet, what is of outmost importance is that Mikhail is now more aware and conscious of his unexplained preoccupation with these distant women:

> Who was she?
>
> Why did it concern me? And why did I care what she did in life, who she was, what her relationships, what her circumstances, whether she was a teacher at the primary school attached to the Anglican Church where my sister Louisa studied? I did not ask her. Was she a sales girl in a department store? Did she work at the mill with Mona's sister Gamalat? Was she married or not? (al-Kharrat 1993, 55-56)

Mikhail has departed from mere observation and preoccupation with women and ponders the significance of women for him: "Why did it concern me?" Indeed, he begins to realize the catalytic effect that they have on his emotional and spiritual existence. This realization puzzles him yet it does not deter him from continuing to pose to himself the question of why women are so significant in his life:

> But I knew that she was neither single nor married, she was beyond that, she was not subject to the laws of this earth. (ibid., 56)

> The fire of her eyes in mine, just for an instant. The shadow of a faint illusory smile, almost imperceptible. Every day. Every morning. (ibid.)

The identity of each woman is not as important as Mikhail's recollection of them is and of what each of them signifies for him. The "she" that Westney Gaze refers to and the Gravesian "other woman" both lack a clear and fixed identity.

> Whether she exists or is a figment of his imagination is never quite clear – nor is it clear whether he is writing about one woman or a composite of many. At other times Alexandria seems to be the beloved. (Deeb 1990, 730)

"She" can be Alexandria signifying the hero's/narrator's memories which are as liminal and as intangible as the girls of the city. Through the one Alexandria and its many women, the hero/narrator attempts to reconnect with a part of himself that he has lost yet still exists in his mind and consciousness:

> The return to the "lost places of boyhood and youth resurrected from their deep grave" paradoxically testifies to the impossibility of such a return, for each memory in *Girls of Alexandria* is at once an exhilarating moment of recovery and a desolate moment of irrevocable loss. (Amireh 1994, 627)

The "lost places of boyhood and youth" echo the "distant regions" of the White Goddess, and Alexandria becomes the unifying thread that reconnects the narrator with his anima.

For al-Kharrat, as well as for Graves, femininity and liminality are inextricably connected and constitute a significant source of inspiration and creativity. The liminal and mysterious elements surrounding femininity are an endless creative challenge for the perennial Gravesian poet who finds his incarnation in al-Kharrat's young Mikhail. For Mikhail this challenge is not only intellectual and spiritual but also, and most significantly, existential.

WORKS CITED

Abulafia, David. 2011. *The Great sea: A human history of the Mediterranean*. Oxford and New York: Oxford University Press.

Alberich, J. 1965. El erotismo femenino en el teatro de García Lorca. *Papeles de son Armadams* 3-36.

Alridge, Owen A. 1969. *Comparative literature: Matter and method. Urbana: University of Illinois Press.*

Allen, Rupert. 1974. *Psyche and symbol in the theater of Federico García Lorca, Perlimplin, Yerma, Blood Wedding*. Austin and London: University of Texas Press.

Amireh, Amal. 1994. Girls of Alexandria. *World Literature Today* 68 (3): 627-628.

Apollonius Rhodius. 1912. *Argonautica.* Book III. London: Heineman.

Arnott, Peter D. 1977. *An introduction to the French theatre*. London: Macmillan.

Arthur, Marylin. 1977. Politics and pomegranates: An interpretation of the Homeric Hymn to Demeter. *Arethusa* 10:7-47.

Arturi Parilla, Catherine. 1995. *A theory for reading dramatic texts, Selected plays by Pirandello and García Lorca*. New York and Washington: Peter Lang.

Ballas, Shimon. 1993. The circular structure of Edwar Al-Kharrat's work: An approach to *Mahattat al-Sikkah al-Hadid* ('The railway Station'). In *Writer, Culture, Text*, ed. A. Elad, 26-36. Canada: York Press.

Barea, Arturo. 1994. *Lorca, the poet and his people*. London: Faber and Faber.

Barthes, Roland. 1964. *On Racine*. Trans. Richard Howard. New York: Hill and Wang.

Beaton, Roderick. 1999. *An introduction to modern Greek literature*, 2nd ed. Oxford: Clarendon Press.

Bergson, Henri. 1935. *The two sources of morality and religion*. New York: Henry Holt and Company.

Blumenberg, Hans. 1990. *Work on myth*. Trans. Robert M. Wallace Cambridge, MA and London: MIT Press.

Boewe , Charles. 1961. Myth and Literary Studies. *University of Kansas City Review* 27 (3): 191-196.

Booth, Alison. 1996. Abduction and Other Severe Pleasures: Rita Dove's *Mother Love. Callaloo* 19 (1): 125-130.

Bowra, C. M. 1969. The simplicity of Racine. In *Racine: Modern judgements*, ed. R. C. Knight, 36-40. London: Macmillan.
Braudel, Fernand. 2002. M*emory and the Mediterranean*. New York: Vintage.
Butler, Philip. 1974. *Racine: A study*. London: Heinemann.
Carter, D. N. 1989. *Robert Graves: The lasting poetic achievement*. London: Macmillan.
Cassirer, Ernst. 1945. *An essay on man: An introduction to a philosophy of human culture*. New Haven: Yale University Press.
—. 1964. *The philosophy of symbolic forms.* Vol. 2: *Mythical Thought.* New Haven and London: Yale University Press.
Chambers. Ian. 2008. *Mediterranean Crossings: The Politics of an Interrupted Modernity*. Durham, NC: Duke University Press.
Cleasby, Loomis Harold. 1907. The Medea of Seneca. *Harvard Studies in Classical Philology* 18: 39-71.
Cohen, J. M. 1963. *Robert Graves*. Edinburgh and London: Oliver and Boyd.
Correa, Gustavo. 1962. Honor, Blood, and Poetry in *Yerma. Tulane Drama Review* 7 (2): 96-110.
—. 1957. *La poesia mitica de Federico García Lorca*. Eugene Oregon: University of Oregon Publications.
Dahl, Curtis. 1958. A Double Frame for Tennyson's Demeter? *Victorian Studies* 1: 357-362.
Day, Douglas. 1963. *Swifter that reason: The poetry and criticism of Robert Graves*. Chapel Hill: The University of North Carolina Press.
DeBloois, Nanci.1997. Rape, marriage, or death? Gender perspectives in the Homeric Hymn to Demeter. *Philological Quarterly* 76 (3): 245-262.
Deeb, Mary-Jane. 1990. City of Saffron. *Middle East Journal* 44 (4) (Autumn): 730.
Degoy, Susana. 1999. *En lo mas oscuro del pozo: figura y rol de la mujer en el teatro de García Lorca*. Granada: Ediciones Miguel Sanchez.
De Mourgues, Odette. 1967. *Racine or the triumph of relevance*. London and New York: Cambridge University Press.
Douglas, Wallace W. 1996. The Meanings of 'Myth' in Modern Criticism. In *Literary Criticism and Myth 4* Ed. Robert Segal. New York and London: Garland Publishing.
Dove, Rita, in www.heinzawards.net/recipients/rita-dove (accessed November 3, 2014)
—. 1995. *Mother love*. New York: Norton.
Edwards, Gwynne. 1980. *Lorca: The theatre beneath the sand.* London and Boston: Marion Boyars.

Euripides. 1958. Medea. In *Three great plays of Euripides*. Trans. Rex Warner. New York: Mentor.

—. 1995. Hippolytus. In *Children of Heracles, Hippolytus, Andromache, Hecuba*. Trans and ed. David Kovacs. The Loeb Classical Library. Cambridge, MA and London: Harvard University Press, 123- 263.

Felson-Rubin, Nancy and Deal Harriet M. 1994. Some functions of the Demophoon episode in the Homeric Hymn to Demeter. In *The Homeric hymn to Demeter: Translation, commentary and interpretative essays,* ed. Helen P. Foley. New Jersey: Princeton University Publications, 190-197.

Fernández-Cifuentes, Luis. 1984. Yerma: Anatomia de una transgresion. *Modern Language Notes* 16 (2) (March): 288-307.

Frankfort, H and H.A. 1948. 'Myth and Reality' in *The intellectual adventure of ancient man: An essay on speculative thought in the ancient Near East*, ed. H&H.A et al., Chicago: The University of Chicago Press.

Gersting, Judith L. 1998. *Mathematical structures for computer science.* New York: W.H. Freeman.

Glezos, Petros. 1981. Ο Μ. Καραγάτσης ως διηγηματογράφος [M. Karagatsis as a short story writer]. *Τετράδια Ευθύνης* 14: 27-32.

Glover, J. 1996. *Mother Love* - Rita Dove. *Stand* 38 (Winter): 81

Graves, Robert. 1948. *The white goddess*. London: Faber and Faber.

—. 1949. *The common asphodel: collected essays on poetry (1922-1949).* London: Harnish Hamilton.

—. 1958. *Five pens in hand*. New York: Doubleday.

—. 1962. *Oxford addresses on poetry*. London: Cassell.

—. "Where the crakeberries grow: Robert Graves gives an account of himself to Leslie Norris" in http:www.lib.byu.edu/~english/wwI/influence/graves.html

—. 1965. *Mammon and the black goddess.* London: Cassell.

—. 1967. *Poetic craft and principle*. London: Cassell.

—. 1970. ('Where the crakeberries grow – Robert Graves gives an account of himself to Leslie Norris', *Listener*, 28 May http://www.lib.buy.edu/~english/wwwI/influence/graves.html (accessed 3 March, 2014)

—. 1975. *Collected poems. London: Cassell.*

—. 1987. *The Greek myths,* Vol. 2. London: Penguin Books.

—. 1997. *The white Goddess.* Ed. Grevel Lindop. London: Faber and Faber.

—. 1923. What is Bad Poetry? *North American Review* 218 (July/ December): 353-368.

Greenfield, Sumner M. 1981. Yerma, The woman and the work: some reconsiderations. *Estreno* 7: 18-21.

Guillen, Claudio. 1993. *The challenge of comparative literature*. Massachusetts and London: Harvard University Press.

Hammond, M. 2000. Subsuming the feminine other: Gender and narration in Idwar Al-Kharrat's *Ya banat Iskandariyya. Journal of Arabic Literature* 31 (1): 38-58.

Haris, Petros. 1981. *Σαράντα χρόνια κριτικής ελληνικού πεζού λόγου, 1928-1949*. [Forty years of criticism in greek prose 1928-1949]. Αθήνα: Ελληνικό Λογοτεχνικό και Ιστορικό Αρχείο.

Harris, W.V. Ed. 2005a. *Rethinking the Mediterranean*, Oxford: Oxford University Press.

—. 2005b. The Mediterranean and Ancient History. In *Rethinking the Mediterranean*, ed. W.V. Harris, Oxford: Oxford University Press.

Horden, Peregrine. 2005. Mediterranean excuses: Historical writing on the Mediterranean since Braudel. *History and Anthropology* 16 (1) (March): 25-30.

Horden Peregrine and Purcell Nicholas. 2000. *The Corrupting Sea: A Study of Mediterranean History*. Oxford and Massachusetts: Blackwell.

Irwin, Robert. 1989. The knowledge of secrets. *Times Literary Supplement*, 4511 (15th Sept.).

James, E.D., and Jondorf, G. 1994. *Racine Phèdre*. Cambridge: Cambridge University Press.

Jordan, Elaine. 1988. *Alfred Tennyson*. Cambridge: Cambridge University Press.

Jung, C.G., and C. Kerenyi. 1970. *Introduction to a science of Mythology: the myth of the divine child and the mysteries of Eleusis.* London: Routledge and Kegan.

Karagatsis, M. 1992. *Ή μεγάλη χίμαιρα* [The great chimera]. Athens: Hestia.

Karantonis, Antreas. 1977. *Νεοελληνική λογοτεχνία: φυσιογνωμίες* [Modern Greek literature: Figures]. Vol. 2. Athens: Papadimas.

Karouzos, N.D. 1981. Μ. Καραγάτσης [M. Karagatsis]. *Τετράδια Ευθύνης* 14: 47-48

Keane, Patrick J. 1980. *A wild civility: interactions in the poetry and thought of Robert Graves*. Columbia: University of Missouri Press.

Kerenyi, Carl. 1970. 'Prolegomena' In *Introduction to a science of mythology, The Myth of the Divine Child and the Mysteries of Eleusis*. London: Routledge and Kegan.

al-Kharrat, Idwar. *City of saffron*. 1989. London: Quartet Books.

—. *Girls of Alexandria*. 1993. London: Quartet Books.

—. 1998. Random variations on an autobiographical Theme. In *Writing the self: Autobiographical writing in modern arabic literature*. ed. R. Ostle et al., 9-17. London: Saqi Books

Kirk, S. G. 1973. *Myth: its meaning and functions in ancient and other cultures*. Cambridge: Cambridge University Press.

Kirkham, Michael. 1969. *The poetry of Robert Graves*. London: Athlone, University of London Press.

Kitto, H.D.F. 1993. *Greek tragedy*, A literary study. London: Routledge.

Knox, Bernard. 1979. *Word and action: essays on the ancient theater*. Baltimore and London: John Hopkins Press.

Kokkinaki, Nena. 1991. Η αντινομία του ήθους στον Καραγάτση [The contradiction of morality in Karagatsis]. *Διαβαζω* 258 (6th March): 56-59.

Kohli, Derindra. 1974. *The necessary trance: conflict and liberation in the poetry of Robert Graves*. PhD Thesis, University of Leeds.

Kottaridou, Angeliki. Ed. 1995. *Από τη Μήδεια στη Σαπφώ: Ανυπότακτες γυναίκες στην αρχαία Ελλάδα* [From Medea to Sappho: Unsubjugated women in ancient Greece]. Athens: Athina.

Kovacs, David. 1987. *The heroic muse: studies in the Hippolytus and Hecuba of Euripides.* Baltimore and London: John Hopkins University Press.

Lacalle Martínez, Guadalupe. 1988. Yerma: Una tragedia pura y simplemente. *Neophilologus* 72 (2): 227-237.

Lapp, John C. 1955. *Aspects of Racinian tragedy*. Toronto: University of Toronto Press.

Lee, Jane. 1996. Gide, Phèdre, classicism and passion. A fresh interpretation of a guilty passion. In *The literary potrayal of passion through the ages, An interdisciplinary view*, ed. Keith Cameron. New York: The Edwin Mellen Press.

Lépine, Jacques-Jude. 1994. Phaedra's labyrinth as the paradigm of passion: Racine's aesthetic formulation of mimetic desire. *Contagion: Journal of violence, mimesis and culture* 1 (Spring): 47-62.

Lesky, Albi. 1965. *Greek tragedy*. Trans. H. A. Frankfort. London: Ernest Benn.

Lima, Robert. 1963. *The theatre of García Lorca*. New York: Las Americas Publishing Company.

Lofgren, Lotta. 1996. Partial horror: fragmentation and healing in Rita Dove's *Mother Love*. *Callaloo* 19 (1): 135-142.

Lorca, Federico García. 1976. *Yerma.* In *Federico García Lorca: collected plays*. Trans. James, Graham-Lujan and Richard L. O'Connell. London: Secker and Warburg.

—. 1956. *Yerma.* In *Lorca: Obras completas* [Lorca: Complete works]. Ed. Guillermo de Torre. Buenos Aires: Editorial Losada.

Lotan, Yael. 1962. *Phaedra*. New York: Bantam Books.

Luschnig, C. A. E. 1988. *Time holds the mirror: A study of knowledge in Euripides' Hippolytus.* Mnemosyne: Biblioteca Classica Batava. Leiden: E. J. Brill.

—. 1983. The value of ignorance in the Hippolytus. *American Journal of Philology* 104 (2) (Summer): 115-123.

Mabrey, Maria Cristina C. 1996. La sexualidad femenina contra la estructura de poder en *Yerma* de F.G.Lorca. *Hispanofila* 116: 35-45.

Machado Bonet de Benvenuto, Ofelia. 1951. *Federico García Lorca, Su produccion dramatica*. Montevideo: Imprenta Rosgal.

Macpherson Ian and Jaqueline Minett. 1987. Eds. and trans. *Yerma*. Warminster: Aris and Phillips.

McDonald, Marianne. 1997. Medea as politician and diva: Riding the dragon into the future. In *Medea: Essays on Medea in myth, literature, philosophy and art.* Ed. James J. Clauss and Sarah Iles, Johnston. New Jersey: Princeton University Press.

Meletinsky, Eleazar M. 1998. *The poetics of myth*. New York and London: Routledge.

Meraklis, M. G. 1981. Τρεις παραγραφοι της Καραγατσικης πεζογραφιας (Three paragraphs of Karagatsean prose). *Τετράδια Ευθύνης* 14: 53-63.

Merritt, Frederick S. 1962. *Mathematics manual: methods and principles of the various branches of Mathematics for reference, problem solving and review.* New York: McGraw-Hill.

Meyer, Stefan G. 2001. *The experimental Arabic novel: postcolonial literary modernism in the Levant*. New York: State University of New York Press.

Mitta, Dimitra. 1997. *Απολογία για τον μύθο* [An Apology for Myth]. Thessaloniki: University Studio Press.

Mitsakis, K. 1977. *Νεοελληνική πεζογραφία: η γενιά του '30* [Modern Greek prose: the generation of the '30s]. Athens: Ellinini Paideia.

Morse, Ruth. 1996. *The medieval Medea*. Cambridge: D. S. Brewer.

Murray, Gilbert. 1913. *Euripides and his age.* London: Williams and Norgate.

Nath, Santosh. 1992. *Treatment of Greek mythology in the poems of Tennyson*. Aligarh: Printwell Publications.

Nussbaum, C. Martha. 1997. Serpents in the soul: A reading of Seneca's *Medea*. In *Medea: Essays on Medea in myth, literature, philosophy and art*, ed. James J. Clauss and Sarah Iles Johnston, 219-249. New Jersey: Princeton University Press.

O'Prey, Paul. 2001.Out of time: Robert Graves in perspective. *PN Review* (November-December): 42-45.

—. 1982. *In broken images: selected letters of Robert Graves, 1914-1946*. London: Hutchinson.

Padel, Ruth. 1995. *Whom gods destroy: elements of Greek and tragic madness*. Princeton and New Jersey: Princeton University Press.

Page, D. L. 1988. Ed. *Medea* by Euripides with introduction and comments. Oxford: Clarendon Press.

Palaska, Maria. 2014. The ultimate trench: Poetic consciousness and the experience of war. *Gravesiana* 4 (1) (Summer): 150-161.

Papaditsas Dimitris and Eleni Ladia. Trans and eds.1997. Εἰς Δημήτραν [To Demeter]. In *Ομηρικοί ύμνοι* [Homeric Hymns]. Athens: Hestia.

Pater, Walter. 1922. *Greek studies*. London: Macmillan.

Paul, Georgina. 1997. Schwierigkeiten mit der dialektik: zu Christa Wolf's *Medea: Stimmen*. *German Life and Letters* 5 (2): 227-240.

Pittas-Herschbach, Mary. 1990. *Time and space in Euripides and Racine*. New York: Peter Lang.

Pocock, Gordon. 1973. *Corneille and Racine: problems of tragic form*. Cambridge: Cambridge University Press.

Politis, Linos. 1973. *A history of modern Greek literature*. Oxford: Clarendon Press.

Powell, Neil. 1997. Leaving the rest unsaid. *Poetry Review* 87 (4): 88-89.

Predrag, Matvejevic. 1999. *Mediterranean: a cultural landscape*.Trans. Michael Henry Heim. Berkeley: University of California Press

Purcell, Nicholas. 2003. The boundless sea of unlikeness: on defining the Mediterranean. *Mediterranean Historical Review* 18 (2) (December): 9-29.

Rabinowitz Sorkin, Nancy. 1987. Female speech and female sexuality: Euripides *Hippolytos* as model. In *Rescuing Creusa: New methodological approaches to women on antiquity*. Ed. Marilyn Skinner. A Special Issue of Helios, New Series, 13 (2), Lubbock: Texas Tech University Press, 127-140.

Racine, Jean. 1970. *Iphigenia, Phaedra, Athaliah*. Trans. John Cairncross. London: Penguin Books.

—. 1980. *Theatre complet*. Ed. Jacques Morel and Alain Viala. Paris: Editions Garnier Freres.

Ricks, Christopher. 1972. *Tennyson*. London and New York: Macmillan.

Rooksby, Rikky. 1984. 'A Graves Revision.' *English Language Notes* 21 (3): 53-57.

Sanders, Peter L. 1970. Robert Graves - A Poet's Quest for Meaning. *English Journal* (National Council of Teachers of English, Urbana, Illinois) 59 (1): 23-26.

Sargent Thelma. Trans. 1975. Homeric Hymn to Demeter. In *The Homeric hymns: A verse translation*. New York and London: Norton.

Seneca, 1960. Medea In *Seneca's tragedies* Vol.1. Trans. F.J. Miller, London: Heinemann.

Scarborough Milton. 1994. *Myth and modernity*. Albany: State University of New York Press.

Schultz, William. 2000. *Cassirer and Langer on myth: an introduction*. New York and London: Garland.

Segal, Charles. 1988. Confusion and concealment in Euripides' *Hippolytus.*Vision, hope, and tragic knowledge. *Mètis Anthropologie des mondes grecs anciens* 3 (1-2): 263-282

Segal, Robert A. 2004. *Myth: a very short introduction*. Oxford: Oxford University Press.

Seymour-Smith, Martin. 1982. *Robert Graves: his life and work.* London: Hutchinson.

Shafi, Monika. 1997. "Falsch leiden sollte es das auch geben": Konfliktstrukturen in Christa Wolf's roman *Medea. Colloquia Germanica* 30 (4): 375-385.

Shaw, D. C. 1980. The ambiguity of Phedre. *Nottingham French Studies* 19 (1): 46-58.

Snipes, Katherine. 1979. *Robert Graves*. New York: Frederick Ungar Publishing.

Sourvinou-Inwood, Christiane. 1997. Medea at a shifting distance: Images and Euripidean tragedy. In *Medea: Essays on Medea in myth, literature, philosophy and art,* ed. James J. Clauss and Sarah Iles, Johnston, 254-296. New Jersey: Princeton University Press.

Spoerri, Theophil. 1969. Racine: Impulse and mind. In *Racine: Modern judgements,* ed. R. C. Knight. Great Britain: Macmillan.

Stade, George. 1967 'Robert Graves.' In *Columbia Essays on Modern Writers* No 25, New York & London: Columbia University Press.

Steiner, George. 1960. The genius of Robert Graves. *Kenyon Review* 22 (3) (Summer): 340-365.

Stambovsky, Phillip. 1996. *Myth and the limits of reason*. Amsterdam and Atlanta: Rodopi.

Tennyson, Alfred Lord. 1892. 'Demeter and Persephone' In *Demeter and other poems,* (2nd ed.) London: Macmillan, 1892.

Tennyson, Hallam. ed. 1897. *Alfred Lord Tennyson: a memoir by his son*. Vol. 2. London: Macmillan.

Terencio, Yolanda. 1993. *Ο κόσμος χτες-σήμερα-αύριο: άνθρωποι του πνεύματος* [The world yesterday-today-tomorrow: men of intellect] Athens: Minoas.

Tubert, S. 1993. The deconstruction and construction of maternal desire, *Yerma* and *Die Frau ohne Schatten. Mosaic, A Journal for the interdisciplinary study of literature* 26 (3): 69-87.

Turnell, Martin. 1971. *The Classical moment, Studies of Corneille, Moliere and Racine*. Connecticut: Greenwood Press.

—. 1972. *Jean Racine dramatist*. Great Britain and New York: New Directions.

Turner, Barbara. 1999. Christa Wolf's Medea: Stimmen. In *Placing classical Greek theatre,* ed. Savas Patsalidis and Elisabeth Sakellaridou. Thessaloniki: University Studio Press.

Tzoulis, Thanassis, X. 1993. Η ανάγκη και η επιθυμία στο έργο του Μ. Καραγάτση. *Ψυχανάλυση και λογοτεχνία*. [Necessity and need in the M. Karagatsis's oeuvre]. Athens: Odysseas.

Vickery, John. 1972. *Robert Graves and the White Goddess*. Lincoln: University of Nebraska Press.

—. 1996. Literature and Myth. In *Theories of myth: From ancient Israel and Greece to Freud, Jung, Campbell and Levi-Strauss,* IX *Literary Criticism and Myth*, ed. Robert A. Segal, 283-303. New York & London: Garland Publishing, 1996.

Vinaver, E. 1969. Action and poetry in Racine's tragedies. In *Racine: Modern judgements*, ed. R. C. Knight. London: Macmillan.

Ward, Scott. 1995. No vers is libre. *Shenandoach* 45 (3) (Fall): 107-119.

Webster, T. B. L. 1967. *The tragedies of Euripides*. London: Methuen.

Weimer, Christopher Brian. 1992. Journeys from frustration to empowerment: *Cat on a hot tin roof* and its debt to García Lorca's *Yerma. Modern Drama* 35 (4): 520-529.

Weinberg, Bernard. 1963. *The art of Jean Racine*. Chicago and London: The University of Chicago Press.

Westney, Emma Gaze. 2000. *Arabic literary modernism: the short story cycles and episodic novels of Imil Habibi and Idwar al-Kharrat* (PhD Thesis), Oxford: University of Oxford.

Wolf, Christa. 1999. *Medea: Stimmen.* New York: Virago Press.

Wolf, Christa, 'From Cassandra to Medea: Impulses and Motives Behind My Work on Two Mythical Figures', Interview in www.randomhouse.com/boldtype/0498/wolf/notebook.html (accessed 3 March 2014)

Yarrow, P. J. 1978. *Racine*. Oxford: Blackwell.

Zeitlin, Froma. 1996. *Playing the other: gender and society in classical Greek literature*. Chicago and London: The University of Chicago Press.

Ziolkowski, Eric. J. 1996. Sancho Panza and Nemi's priest: Reflections on the relationship of literature and myth. In *Myth and method*, ed. Laurie Pattan and Wendy Doniger, 247-291. Charlottesville and London: University Press of Virginia.

INDEX